Praise for *Between Fathers & Daughters* ❖

Fathers and daughters who are trying to understand each other and build a better relationship can do no better than *Between Fathers and Daughters*. Among the lessons they'll learn is that mutual understanding is often blocked by cultural messages that demean fathers and idealize mothers. Daughters who have taken Nielsen's class are surprised to learn how they've been misled by mass media; fathers are grateful when they do.

—Kathleen Parker, syndicated columnist
and author of *Save the Males*

Remarkable! This book is amazing—thoughtfully weaving together research findings, common sense advice, principles of psychotherapy, and personal stories into a compelling work that has immense promise to alleviate the weight and pain of daughters being estranged from their fathers. Presuming to speak on behalf of the fathers to whom you will restore the great gift of their daughters, "Thank you!"

—Sanford Braver, PhD, Arizona State University,
author of *Divorced Dads: Shattering the Myths*
and advisor to President Clinton's Fatherhood Initiative

To say we love without knowing what we are loving is a wasted life. To discover our dad's or our daughter's love is to discover both them and ourselves. Nielsen's book guides us to both by data that makes us question what we know, by insights that help us discover what we don't know, and with questionnaires that help us understand ourselves. Every dad and daughter must read it.

—Warren Farrell, author of *Father and Child Reunion*
and *Why Men Are the Way They Are*

A masterful book written in a disarmingly casual conversational style—with more than two hundred heavy-duty citations to entice the academic community as well. With a lovely blend of anecdotal stories, crisp statistical summaries, and handy self-test quizzes, the author clearly understands communication. The chapter on divorced father-daughter relationships is superb and worth the price of the book alone.

—Canadian Equal Parenting Council

Professor Nielsen writes with more wisdom, experience, and care about this than anyone else out there. If you are a father or a daughter, or someone who cares about a daughter and father, get this book!

—Joshua Coleman, PhD, senior fellow,
Council on Contemporary Families and author of
*When Parents Hurt: Compassionate Strategies When
You and Your Grown Child Don't Get Along*

Nielsen's book breaks new ground by including men as significant parents. Fathers are and should be encouraged to think of themselves as more than just the "stranger who signs the checks." Read this book!

—Karen DeCrow, attorney and former
president of the National Organization of Women

Dr. Nielsen brilliantly brings home the facts about what really happens in families of divorce and offers practical solutions. Research and real-life stories are combined with interesting and thought-provoking quizzes and self-tests. Her practical insights and recommendations will bring understanding and healing for all who dare to look.

—Maureen Geddes and Bob McGuire,
co-presidents, Canadian Equal Parenting Council

Nielsen banishes all excuses with this practical blueprint for renewal. This book provided a set of useful strategies even for me, a father of six spectacular daughters.

—Rabbi Daniel Lapin, founder of American
Alliance of Jews and Christians

Dr. Linda Nielsen is at the vanguard of educators and authors who know that the father-daughter relationship is fundamental and critical to the development of whole, healthy women. Nielsen's work deserves our unending gratitude.

—Jonetta Rose Barras, columnist, political analyst,
and author of *Whatever Happened to Daddy's Little Girl?*

Girls with loving, involved fathers flourish and become strong, secure women. Based on years of experience and recent research, Dr. Linda Nielsen's book tells fathers and daughters in any family situation how to nurture this core relationship.

—Elizabeth Marquardt, Institute of American Values,
author of *Between Two Worlds: The Inner Lives of Children of Divorce*

Between Fathers and Daughters is an insightful, powerful work that gets beyond the stereotypes to provide a real-world examination of a tremendously underrated relationship.

—Glenn Sacks, men's columnist and radio host of *His Side*

Nielsen identifies the fears, hurts, and anger that separate fathers and daughters and—more important—she gives powerful tools to move beyond the past. Stop feeling sorry for yourself, stop feeling angry, and get moving before it is too late with Nielsen's expert advice.

—Richard A. Warshak, PhD, author of *Divorce Poison: Protecting the Parent-Child Bond from a Vindictive Ex*

Linda Nielsen's work on healing the father-daughter relationship gives me hope for the future. At a time when healthy family ties are more necessary than ever, Nielsen's compassionate treatment of the experiences of both father and daughter is nothing short of revolutionary.

—Rebecca Walker, author of *Black White and Jewish: Autobiography of a Shifting Self* and *Baby Love*

Wow! Dr. Nielsen's no-nonsense, fair-minded, and loving approach shows both daughter and dad positive paths to a strong relationship—a relationship that isn't dependent on denigrating mothers or believing myths about how families work. This is a landmark book.

—Joe Kelly, president of Dads and Daughters and author of *Dads and Daughters*

Between
Fathers & Daughters

Between
Fathers & Daughters

Enriching and Rebuilding Your Adult Relationship

Linda Nielsen, EdD

CUMBERLAND HOUSE

NASHVILLE, TENNESSEE

BETWEEN FATHERS & DAUGHTERS
Published by Cumberland House Publishing, Inc.
431 Harding Industrial Drive
Nashville, Tennessee 37211

Cover design by The DesignWorks Group

Library of Congress Cataloging-in-Publication Data
Nielsen, Linda.
 Between fathers & daughters : enriching and rebuilding your adult relationship / Linda Nielsen.
    p. cm.
 Includes bibliographical references and index.
  ISBN 978-1-58182-661-6 (pbk.)
1. Fathers and daughters. 2. Parent and adult child. 3. Fathers—Psychology. 4. Adult children—Family relationships. 5. Adult children—Psychology. I. Title. II. Title: Between fathers and daughters.

HQ755.86N54 2008
646.7'8—dc22

                                                                    2008025424

Printed in the United States of America
1 2 3 4 5 6 7 8 9 10—12 11 10 09 08

In memory of my father, Nils Nielsen

Contents ◆

Acknowledgments

Many talented, energetic people have helped bring this book into being. My agent, Laurie Markusen, has been enthusiastic and supportive from the outset. Laurie found the perfect home for my book at Cumberland House Publishing, with its incredible team: Ron Pitkin, publisher; Paul Mikos, associate publisher; Chris Bauerle, marketing director; Jennifer Behar, publicist; Lisa Taylor, editor; and Billie Brownell, copy editor.

I am indebted to the hundreds of fathers and daughters who have sought my advice by e-mail or phone—and the hundreds of students who have been in my Fathers and Daughters course at Wake Forest University. Your questions and personal stories strengthen and renew my dedication to teaching and writing about father-daughter relationships.

Never to be overlooked is my loving sidekick—Chloe, our corgi, who watches patiently as I work, waiting for a tummy rub. Above all, I am grateful to my best friend, most honest critic, and biggest fan—my husband, Steve Mizel.

Between
Fathers & Daughters

Why Bother? 1

❖

Is This Book for You?

Is this the book for you? You picked it up. You're curious. But why? Maybe because your father-daughter relationship needs a little tune-up. It's not a broken-down wreck, but still, there are certain things that continue to cause tension between you. Even though you love each other, you don't really know each other that well—at least not like two grown-ups in an open, personal friendship. Maybe you're not comfortable spending time together without anyone else around. In fact, maybe you never spend one-on-one time together. Why? Is it because you don't quite know what to talk about, other than the superficial stuff? So you're curious about this book because you know that you could be getting more out of your relationship. Things might be just a little out of whack, but you're willing to learn some new ways to enrich your relationship. But how?

Or maybe your relationship needs a major overhaul. There's so much stress, anger, and distance between you that you're not sure if your relationship needs to go to a repair shop or a junkyard. Or maybe you haven't had contact for so long that you're wondering if anything can make a difference at this point. Still, in the back of your mind there's that hopeful little voice, *maybe, just maybe, there is still hope.* And in your heart, there's an even bigger voice, *I do still care about this relationship. I do want to rebuild.* But how?

This book is going to show you how—regardless of the shape your relationship is in. It doesn't matter if you have a pretty good relationship that just needs a little touch-up here and there or a pretty bad relationship that needs rebuilding from the ground up. You can apply my ideas either way. And in those rare cases where your bond can't be reestablished, you'll learn how to deal with that heartbreaking reality. You will come to understand why you have the kind of relationship you do—both its strengths and its weaknesses. You'll learn what you can say and do to enhance or to rebuild your connection. You'll see the patterns that may be weakening or destroying it, and you'll see how to change those patterns to get more of what you want.

For many of you, this book will be your guide upriver. Your relationship is at risk from dealing with crisis after crisis—an increasing number of obstacles that never seem to end. It reminds me of the story about two people sitting in a field beside a stream one sunny afternoon. Let's assume these people are the two of you. Suddenly, you notice a baby floating in the middle of the stream. One of you jumps in and saves the baby. But as soon as you lay the baby safely on the ground, you see two more babies floating downstream. Again, you jump in and rescue the babies. But as soon as you lay those two babies safely on the ground, you see even *more* babies floating downstream—this time it's five babies! And you think you see even more farther upstream. You start to panic because you can't save so many babies at one time. The mistake you might make is to keep sitting on the bank and frantically jumping in to save as many babies as you can when they float by. But what you need to do is rush upstream, find out who is throwing the babies in the river, and put an end to this. In the same way, your father-daughter bond can't always survive crisis after crisis. To save it, you need to rush upstream and discover the source of the problem so you can put an end to it.

That's what this book is for—to help the two of you get to the root of what is keeping you from being as close as you'd like to be.

Is It Too Late?

Whether you want minor improvements or major ones, you might be wondering, *Is it too late? Are we too old now, too set in our ways, or too damaged by what has already happened?* Possible, but not likely. You can't allow yourself to be ruled by the voice inside you that says, *We can never escape the past.* People can and do overcome things they have said and done to people they love. Take heart from what these fathers and daughters say about following my advice:

> *"The mere mention of my father used to reduce me to tears. I never expected to be shown a way to remedy this ache. But now we're spending time together."*
>
> *"I'm just a random person who was searching on the Internet for a way to make things better with my daughter. I didn't think anyone understood what I was going through. This book has been the tool kit I needed."*
>
> *"I had no idea how to reconnect with my daughter since we hadn't spoken for so long. But Nielsen's advice opened the door. My daughter and I are talking again."*

"If it weren't for Dr. Nielsen's work, I still wouldn't be speaking to my dad after not talking to him for eight years since my parents' divorce."

"I couldn't get my daughter to see me as anything other than this critical, uptight tyrant. But I've learned how to give her advice without upsetting her."

"I have really gotten to know my father as more than an extension of my mother."

"This book taught me what my daughter needs and wants from me. There are no words to describe the ecstasy on beginning this reconciliation."

"My daughter would never share anything personal with me. I felt like an outsider in her life. Using Nielsen's suggestions, we're actually talking now about something other than politics and movies."

"How dare you say nice things about fathers! As a dad I have finally found a book that includes my feelings and experiences. You have courageously gone where others fear to tread!"

"Dr. Nielsen helped me jump-start the process of fixing my relationship with my dad after he remarried."

"I could never imagine talking to my dad about anything personal. But now I see my dad as so much more than just my father."

"I'm ashamed of myself now for realizing how unfair I was in judging my father and his motives."

"I have stopped running to mom like a little kid every time I'm upset with dad. I now talk directly to him."

"I used to only think about my father in terms of me and how he affected my life. Now I think about how I affect him."

"I didn't think my dad and I had much to improve on. I was so wrong. I have started getting to know him as a person, and we're actually talking like two grown-ups."

Why Listen to Me?

You may be wondering: *Why should I take advice from this woman? Who is she? How much impact has she had on "real" fathers and daughters?*

Well, I have been teaching, writing, and conducting research on adult daughters' relationships with their fathers for thirty years. As a professor of women's studies and education at Wake Forest University, I have been teaching the only college course in the country devoted exclusively to father-daughter relationships since 1990. Through my university work and counseling, I have developed hundreds of techniques and offered advice that has helped countless fathers and daughters strengthen or rebuild their connection—especially those from divorced families. As you'll see from the stories about real dads and daughters, my advice works.

I'll be sharing dozens of practical techniques that have been very effective in helping others. You'll be taking soul-searching quizzes, doing activities on your own, and having conversations with each other that will deepen your bond and resolve many troubling issues. My advice is also based on hundreds of recent research studies and books by experts other than myself. This research will open your eyes to things you've never considered before. Still, you may be starting out with certain self-defeating beliefs that might prevent you from taking the first step.

Your Relationship: The Far-Reaching Impact

As a dad or a daughter, you know if your relationship needs a major overhaul. There's so much tension or unhappiness between you that both of you—and everyone else in the family—know that your father-daughter bond is hanging by a thread. Throughout this book I'll show you how to weave that fragile thread into a sturdier fabric.

But many fathers and daughters who think their relationship is fine or "okay" the way it is could be getting a lot more from it. You might be one of these fathers and daughters who aren't aware that by making some relatively simple changes you could be getting a lot more joy, comfort, and meaningful experiences from your relationship. So how can you tell if your relationship needs a little tune-up? How do you know if things aren't quite as "fine" as they could be between the two of you? Start by using the "Comfort and Joy" quiz to see how your relationship measures up to what it might become.

Unfortunately some fathers and daughters won't admit that what's going on in their relationship is having a negative impact—not only on each other but also on other aspects of their lives. If this is true for you, then your hidden resentments and feelings of being unloved or unappreciated in your father-daughter relationship are probably spilling over into other parts of your life and having a negative impact on your relationships with spouses, friends, co-workers, and other family members. If the feelings and behaviors in the "Outside Impact" quiz frequently describe you, then take a closer look at your father-daughter relationship to see if that's where your anger, resentment, or feelings of inadequacy might be coming from.

Comfort and Joy

0 = no   1 = somewhat   2 = a lot/definitely

Dad Daughter

____ ____ I really look forward to the time we get to spend together.

____ ____ I feel relaxed and physically at ease when we're together.

____ ____ We feel comfortable giving each other a big hug.

____ ____ We relate like two adults, not like a parent and little kid.

____ ____ We laugh and joke with each other.

____ ____ We can hang out and just "be" with each other.

____ ____ Being together brings out the best in both of us.

____ ____ We've forgiven each other for mistakes we've made in the past.

____ ____ We feel loved and accepted by each other.

____ ____ Our relationship brings me great joy and comfort.

____ ____ **Your score** (20 possible)

QUIZ

The Outside Impact of Your Relationship

Yes or no?

_____ I often feel disappointed or hurt by my friends and loved ones.

_____ I often feel left out, ignored, and unappreciated by others.

_____ I have a lot of physical signs of tension (headaches, neck pain, stomach aches).

_____ I often poke fun or make mean comments about people I care about.

_____ I am jealous of my siblings.

_____ I lose my temper a lot and say things I regret later.

_____ I often feel that my boss or co-workers mistreat me.

_____ I often try to make people feel sorry for me.

_____ I often feel that I just don't measure up to other people.

_____ I often feel that other people don't accept me for who I am.

_____ **Score** (number true out of 10)

By admitting to yourself and to each other that your father-daughter relationship can be improved—and that it might be having a negative impact on other aspects of your life as well—you open yourself up to getting the most out of this book. So let's get started by looking at four foolish beliefs that might be holding you back.

Four Foolish Beliefs

Belief 1: Dad should make the first move because he's older and he's the parent.

In many ways growing older does usually make us wiser. A father probably knows more than his daughter does about planning for retirement, getting ahead in a career, or grilling a steak—all of which require experience, practice, and mistakes. In "practice-makes-perfect" situations, the dad probably should take the first step to point out the problem and suggest ways to fix it. For example, if a dad sees that his daughter is about to burn the steaks or make a bad decision that will affect her financially for years to come, he should definitely take the first step. But your father-daughter relationship isn't like grilling a steak or planning for your financial future. Just because dad is older doesn't necessarily mean that he has more insight than his daughter into what needs fixing in their relationship.

Look at it this way: If you're both stranded at sea in a leaky boat, and if the daughter has been trained to repair boats, why wait for dad to make the first move? Sure, he's older. But he doesn't know squat about repairing boats. This may seem like a silly analogy. But, in fact, in this book you'll discover that dads are often less equipped or less confident than their daughters when it comes to fixing the leaks in a relationship—or steering it back on the right course.

Belief 2: If I take the first step to improve our relationship—or to re-establish contact—it means that most of our problems are my fault. Taking the first step is the same as admitting blame.

Why? Where did you get that goofy idea? I'm sure you can remember times when someone you loved took the first step even though both of you knew the problem was *your* fault, right? I'm sure you were grateful that he or she didn't let their ego or pride stop them from making the first move. As father and daughter, you're both grown-ups. By now neither of you should be naive enough to believe that going first means admitting blame. Little kids might feel and behave this way, but they're children, after all, and you're not.

Belief 3: The person who has done the most damage should make the first move.

Let's leave your father-daughter relationship aside for a minute. Think back to those times when you have hurt someone you loved. Think back to some of the worst mistakes you've made—really big ones. What did you do afterward? Did you feel so ashamed, embarrassed, or guilty that you did nothing at all? Did you ever let months or maybe even years go by without addressing the issue head-on? Did you try to avoid ever bringing it up again? Were you ever afraid to ask the person for a second chance? Ever felt you screwed up so badly that there was no way to make things right again? And have you ever felt grateful or relieved when the injured party made the first move to set things straight? I'm sure you get my point: Often, the person who has damaged a relationship the most has the harder time reaching out, apologizing, or trying to set things right again. But since people have cut you some slack when you behaved like the south end of a northbound mule, why can't you do the same?

Belief 4: Forgiving someone for things he or she did means I have to forget it happened and act as if it had no impact on me.

Nope. Absolutely not. Forgiving does not mean that you have to forget what happened. How could you forget? You've got a brain. And the brain stores memories. Forgiving does not mean that you have to pretend that the other person never hurt your feelings—they did. Forgiving also doesn't mean that you have to act as if what he or she did hasn't had an impact on your relationship. Of course it has, and both of you know it.

But in order to enrich or to rebuild any relationship, you have to do some forgiving. That means being willing to stop punishing the other person for the mistakes that he or she made—stop withholding love, refusing to talk to them, refusing to return their letters or phone calls, or continually reminding them of what they did wrong in the past. Forgiving means being willing to move forward to enjoy whatever the two of you can have from here on—rather than staying stuck in the past. Forgiving is not a gift you give to the other person. It's a gift you give to yourself—the gift of getting whatever pleasure you can from your relationship from this point forward. That gift might turn out to be enormous ongoing joy together for the rest of your lives. Or it might turn out to be just brief moments of joy together from time to time. But if you can't forgive, then your relationship is almost certainly going to stay exactly the way it is. Forgiving is your choice, not the other person's.

Why Try Again?
You may be wondering if you should try again—try to make things better or try to restore your broken bond, especially if you've tried countless times already and made little or no progress. You might figure it's not worth another shot. First, let's consider something that Thomas Edison supposedly said to a young coworker who had given up hope.

"Mr. Edison, I'm sorry to report that we have done one thousand experiments and worked hundreds of hours on this, but we've failed. All our work has been for nothing."

"Nonsense!" Edison replied. "We've made great progress because we've learned a thousand ways in which this will not work."

Like Edison, you've already learned much: You've learned what *not* to say or do again because it hasn't improved your relationship. More important still, odds are that, even though you may have put a lot of time and effort into trying to make things better, you've been using the same techniques and same approaches over and over and over again. But now you are going to learn new approaches. And that can make all the difference.

Can I guarantee that if you follow my advice you'll get exactly the kind of relationship you've always wanted? Of course not. I'd be insulting your intelligence to tell you that any book can transform a relationship into 100 percent perfection. But I can guarantee you this: If you don't try any of my suggestions, you won't get more than what you have now. Think about your situation in terms of how the people in the following parable dealt with their thirst.

The first person is dying of thirst. But she's in luck—she finds a well. Luck again—there's a bucket, a rope, and a hammer nearby. So she picks up the hammer, ties it to the rope, and tries lifting drops of water on the hammer's head. She tries again and again and again. Eventually, she dies of thirst because she can't lift enough drops of water on the hammer to quench her thirst. She never used the bucket. Like her, you too may be using the wrong tools on your relationship. But my book offers new tools—tools that have worked for many other fathers and daughters.

Or are you like this thirsty man? He isn't dying of thirst, but he has a throbbing headache because he's dehydrated. He finds the well and he knows that he has to use the bucket, not the hammer, to get the water. But he's afraid of wells. He almost fell into one when he was a little boy. So he decides to put up with his splitting headache rather than go near that scary well. Of course, what he'd really like is for someone to come along and haul the water out for him. But because he doesn't need the water from the well to survive, he just sits there with a throbbing headache. Like him, maybe you're willing to tolerate the headaches in your relationship because you're too afraid to try for more. If so, my book shows you how to overcome the fears that are limiting your relationship.

But maybe you're like this thirsty father and daughter. They know how to haul the water up with the bucket, and they're not afraid of the well. Unfortunately, the two of them have been seriously injured and they can't bend their elbows. They use their unbending arms to haul up the water, but they can't get the water from the bucket to their lips because their arms won't bend. And the bucket is too small for them to stick their face in to sip the water. They're bound to die.

If you're like these last two, my book is going to teach you how to help each other get more out of your relationship. We don't need perfect conditions to make this happen. You can have broken arms that don't bend at the elbows, so to speak. Here's the solution: If the father and the daughter each lift the bucket straight up with their unbending arms and tilt it toward the other's mouth, they can take turns drinking. They work together to get what they each need and want. My book shows you how to enrich and rebuild *together*.

Five Reasons Not to Read This Book
Having shown how you can benefit from this book, let me point out what can prevent you from getting much out of my advice.

Reason 1: You don't want to change yourself. You want the other person to do the changing.

There's an old joke among therapists that goes: How many psychologists does it take to change a light bulb? Only one, but the light bulb has to *want* to be changed. I don't have the power to make you want to change the way you relate to each other. Nobody has that power, except you. Since you're not a light bulb, you can't be changed by any psychologist or by any book unless you want to change. Change is something you have to do yourself. Most of my advice involves ways of changing yourself, not ways to change other people.

Reason 2: You enjoy blaming other people for the shape your relationship is in.

This book is not about blaming people for their imperfections. Instead, I'm inviting you to focus on things you can do differently. I'm certain that both of you have said and done things over the years that damaged or limited your bond. Okay, so what? As the saying goes, "Nature didn't make any of us perfect, so it did the next best thing by making all of us blind to our own faults." Yes, I am going to help you see the mistakes you've each made in the past. But that's so you won't repeat them—not so you can blame each other. What matters now is to look forward with hope, not backward with blame.

Reason 3: You believe there's little benefit in knowing what the research says about father-daughter relationships. You'd rather rely on your own personal experiences.

In every chapter I explain what our best research has to say about dads and daughters. I do this because there are so many lies and half-truths in our society about fathers—and about father-daughter relationships. And until you can free yourself from those lies and half-truths, you are limiting your relationship from being the best that it can be.

Reason 4: You don't want to talk about anything or do anything that might make you the least bit uncomfortable.

If that's the case, don't read this book. I am going to ask you to step outside your comfort zone and do some things that will initially make you feel awkward or nervous. I'm going to be asking you to try new things and to talk about some difficult topics with each other. You're going to do some work—and some soul-searching. And that's not always going to be comfortable for you.

Reason 5: You're not ready yet to work on the relationship. The timing isn't right.

If that's how you feel, think again: Most men in our country die before the age of eighty-five, seven years sooner than most women. This means that when a daughter is fifty years old, she only has a 50 percent chance that her father will still be alive. I want you to understand how much is at stake here. Your time is running out. There's not going to be a magic moment like in the movies where you will both suddenly realize it's the perfect time to work on your relationship. It's important to come to grips with this. Take a long look at your father-daughter lifeline. If you keep dilly-dallying or making excuses, you may discover that the one thing you need most is the very thing you lack—more time.

Blinding, Binding Beliefs: Fathers Do Matter! 2

❖

Damaging Beliefs

How can certain beliefs about dads and daughters blind and bind you? What have your beliefs got to do with strengthening or rebuilding your relationship? Just this: Negative beliefs about fathers and about father-daughter relationships blind you both because you can't see how much more the two of you really have to offer each other. You can't see how to make your relationship more meaningful, more personal, and more comfortable. You may not even be able to remember the past accurately because your current beliefs are distorting things. Negative beliefs also bind you to think and behave in ways that limit or interfere with your relationship. Beliefs can bind you by making it harder to get the most out of your relationship. Blinding and binding. That's what we're going to explore: How to get your blinders off and how to break free of the beliefs that are holding your relationship back from being all that it can be.

The Media: Demeaning and Denigrating Dads

Your beliefs about fathers and about your relationship have been influenced by what you see and read in the media. And that's bad news because there are far too many myths and half-truths about dads floating around out there. News reports and talk shows often focus on the "bad" dads and ignore the good ones. By pasting together bits and pieces of poorly done or outdated research, by repeatedly citing a single research study, or by sensationalizing a single bad incident as if it represented *most* dads, the media can make a mountain out of a molehill—by adding just enough "dirt."

Commercials often show the dad as the dim-witted doofus who needs his wise wife to show him how to raise the kids. For example, in a 2004 Verizon ad, the computer illiterate dad is humiliated and chewed out by his wife for trying to help their daughter do her homework.[1] Television shows frequently exaggerate the differences between men and women with dad being inferior to mom.[2] Sitcoms typically portray dads as rude, crude, sexist, childish, lazy, and uninterested in their kids.[3] In a 2005 series called *Listen Up*, the dad wears a T-shirt that reads, "I'm only here for the beer." His advice to his clinically depressed teenage daughter is "try to be happier." His son tells the audience what's wrong with dad, "Too much drinkin', not enough thinkin'."[4] Of course, all of us like a good laugh. But if it's laughter we're after, then why aren't mothers being portrayed in equally demeaning ways? Why are we only laughing at fathers? Would we be laughing if any other group of people was always the brunt of the joke? A racial or religious group? Old people?

Likewise in many movies, dad is the birdbrain being manipulated by his daughter into buying her things.[5] The good dad is supposed to be, above all, the "provider"—his daughter's instant cash machine. Academy Award–nominated films typically give us a heavy dose of male characters who are negligent, abusive, alcoholic, adulterous no-goods whose daughters pay a heavy price for dad's behavior.[6] Dads in movies often demean and exploit their daughter, or are sexually attracted to her, or are overbearing when it comes to allowing her to grow up and create her own life with another man.[7] Sadly, too many comic strips and Father's Day cards also reinforce these insulting beliefs about dads.[8, 9] Sadder still, most children's books show dads being far less involved with their kids than moms.[10] I'm waiting for the day when the media and children's book authors treat fathers and mothers equally. In the meantime, be wary of the negative things you read or hear in the media about men as parents.

So what's the big deal? It's a big deal because many fathers seem to buy the media's message that they aren't very good at parenting and that fathers aren't as necessary as mothers. In a 2006 survey nearly 60 percent of fathers felt that they could be replaced by other men in their kids' lives. Poor men were the most likely to feel this way.[11] In a 2004 nationwide poll, one third of fathers said they didn't feel they were terribly necessary or very important in their daughters' lives.[12] It's also a big deal because the media's negative messages influence *your* beliefs—and your beliefs shape the kind of relationship you have created over the years. Let's see how.

Your Family's Beliefs

Let's start by looking at your family's beliefs, some of which may be damaging or interfering with your relationship. Think back to what your family believed while you were growing up as you take the quiz on the following page.

Your Family's Beliefs: Helping or Hurting?

When you were growing up, what did you believe?

0 = strongly agree   1 = agree somewhat
2 = disagree somewhat   3 = strongly disagree

Daughter Dad

_____ _____ Fathers generally have less impact on their daughters than mothers do.

_____ _____ A daughter benefits more from a good relationship with her mom than with her dad.

_____ _____ Mothers know more than fathers about what's good for kids.

_____ _____ Fathers lack the natural instinct that mothers have for raising children.

_____ _____ Mothers sacrifice more than fathers do for their children.

_____ _____ Daughters raised by single moms are better adjusted than those raised by single dads.

_____ _____ Most dads are satisfied with the amount of time they get to spend with their kids.

_____ _____ Most dads are more interested in their jobs than in their kids.

_____ _____ A daughter's relationship with her dad is usually stronger when mom is a housewife.

_____ _____ Moms are more stressed than dads trying to balance work and family.

_____ _____ **Scores** (30 possible)

[22]

The higher your scores, the easier it has been for you to create a comfortable, personal, meaningful father-daughter relationship, and the more in touch you are with what researchers find is true for most families in our country today. As you can see from the research in the "Dad Bashing" section below, none of the beliefs in the quiz is true. On the other hand, the lower your scores, the more likely it is that you don't know each other very well, don't feel comfortable talking about personal things, and don't spend much one-on-one time together. That means the lower your scores, the more your family's beliefs have been limiting your relationship. Let's see how that happens.

Dad Bashing: The Facts

- Daughters raised by single dads are as well adjusted as daughters raised by single moms.[13]
- There is no maternal instinct that makes women better parents than men.[14–16]
- Most dads wish they could spend more time with their kids and less time at work.[17–20]
- Dads and daughters are usually closer when mom works full-time outside the home while the kids are growing up.[21]
- Dads have as much or more impact on their daughters as moms do.[22–23]

The Impact of Your Family's Beliefs

Why does it matter what your family believes about dads and daughters? It matters because your family's beliefs influence the way everyone interacts with one another. And that, in turn, shapes the kind of father-daughter relationship you have developed over the years. Think of it this way: Your family's beliefs are like a movie script. The script tells you what a "normal" or "good" father-daughter relationship is supposed to be. As mom, dad, and daughter, you each act out your parts. But here's the problem: Some parts of the script aren't in the best interests of your relationship. In fact, some parts of the script can be downright devastating in terms of their long-term impact on your relationship.

Let's consider two families' different scripts. In Joan's family, everyone believes that a daughter should have a more open, personal relationship with mom than with dad. Mom and daughter are supposed to spend more one-on-one time together, talk about personal things, and know more about each other's day-to-day lives. Dad, on the other hand, isn't supposed to be interested in the emotional or personal stuff that's going on in his daughter's life. The family script says that because dad is a man, he isn't supposed to talk with his daughter about topics such as sex, dating, boyfriends, female friendships, eating disorders, marriage, his childhood, his problems at work, and his emotions. As for mentioning "female" things like the monthly migraines caused by a daughter's periods, the family believes this is strictly between mother and daughter. Joan's family also believes that mom should raise the kids while dad earns all the money because women have a maternal instinct that men don't have. Especially with girls, moms are better parents than dads.

Now compare this to Roberta's family. Their beliefs have created an entirely different script. Both of her parents believe that a dad should have just as open and as personal a relationship as a mom does with their daughter. When Roberta phones home, she often talks just to her dad, and they talk about things like her boyfriend, problems with her female friends, and her ongoing battle with anxiety. Roberta and her dad often spend time together without mom. When Roberta has monthly migraines with her periods, she is comfortable sending dad to the drugstore to pick up her medicine or whatever else she needs. Two families. Two different belief systems. Two different scripts. Two different outcomes for dad and daughter.

How about your family? How have your beliefs affected your relationship? Daughters, use the "Equal Opportunity Daughters" quiz on page 26 to see the connection between your beliefs and the way you treat your dad. The higher you score, the better your relationship probably is. You've given him equal opportunities to create a relaxed, open, significant relationship with you.

Okay, dads. Now it's your turn. Use the "Equal Opportunity Dads" quiz on page 27 to see how much opportunity you've been giving your daughter to build the strongest possible relationship with you. Have you given her the same chances you've given your son?

The Tricksters: Beliefs, Memory, and Perception

Not only have your beliefs affected the way you treat each other, they have also tricked you into believing things about each other that aren't true. A belief—positive or negative—influences what we do and what we do not remember about the past. Our beliefs also influence how we perceive and interpret what is happening now. If we have a negative opinion of someone, we literally remember more of the negative than the positive things they actually did. In the present, we notice more of the negative things they do and interpret their behavior in a more negative way. In contrast, if we have positive beliefs about a person, we tend to remember mainly the positive

Equal Opportunity Daughters

How do you treat your dad? What beliefs are holding you back?

0 = never   1 = rarely   2 = half the time   3 = almost always

Example:

__1__ I tell my father as much about my personal life as I tell my mother.

My Belief: Men aren't interested in personal or emotional things like women are.

_____ I talk directly to dad instead of going through mom to communicate with him.

My Belief: _____

_____ I go to my father for advice and comfort about personal things.

My Belief: _____

_____ I ask my dad what's going on in his life besides his work.

My Belief: _____

_____ I tell him as much about my day-to-day life as I tell my mother.

My Belief: _____

_____ I ask him to do things alone with me so we have time to talk privately.

My Belief: _____

_____ I have spent just as much time getting to know him as I have my mother.

My Belief: _____

_____ I encourage him to ask me questions about my life.

My Belief: _____

_____ I ask my dad about his life as a child and as a young man.

My Belief: _____

_____ I give him the kinds of presents that show I truly know him.

My Belief: _____

_____ I am as open and honest with dad as I am with mom.

My Belief: _____

_____ **Your score** (30 possible)

Equal Opportunity Dads

How do you relate to your daughter? What beliefs are holding you back?

0 = never   1 = rarely   2 = half the time   3 = almost always

Example:

__1__ I spend time just with her without other family members.

My Belief: Dads aren't supposed to spend time alone with a daughter after she becomes a teenager.

_____ I attend my daughter's events as often as I attend my son's events.

My Belief: _____

_____ I ask her about topics other than school or work.

My Belief: _____

_____ I tell her about specific aspects of my life other than work or sports.

My Belief: _____

_____ I am as open and honest with her as I am with my son.

My Belief: _____

_____ I have spent just as much time getting to know her as I have my son.

My Belief: _____

_____ I know the names of her two closest friends.

My Belief: _____

_____ I encourage her to ask me questions about my life.

My Belief: _____

_____ I have one special activity that I do only with her (such as have breakfast at a certain restaurant, go to a weekly movie, play a silly card game).

My Belief: _____

_____ I tell her that I love her.

My Belief: _____

_____ **Your score** (30 possible)

[27]

things they did in the past. We overlook or "forget" the negative. We're always on the lookout for the good things they do—and give them the benefit of the doubt when they do "not so good" things. These tricksters—beliefs, memories, and perceptions—work as a team. The trickster team influences our memories as well as the meaning and motives we ascribe to everyone's behavior.[24, 25]

If our beliefs about a particular group of people are positive, then our relationship with any member of that group is generally better because we're on the lookout for all the good things they do. We expect the best from them. We look for the best in them. We treat them in ways that bring out the best. But if our beliefs and expectations of a group are negative, then we look for and we find the worst in them. For example, if you believe that mothers are more nurturing than fathers, you will notice and remember more of the nurturing things that moms do and overlook the nurturing things that dads do. Or if you believe that men are less interested in their kids than women are, then you will notice and remember more women showing an interest in kids. You will be far less likely to notice or remember the times you see men showing interest in kids. That's where the old saying comes from: I'll see it *only when* I believe it.

Try the three-day experiment described in the box "Seeing Is Believing, But Are You Blind?" My bet is you're going to start "seeing" things that you never "saw" before. Even when your beliefs about each other aren't true, you can convince yourself that they are.

Your beliefs, memories, and perceptions can damage or limit your relationship. We take whopping liberties with the past. Some of our memories are more reliable than others. But some people—especially those who are extremely dissatisfied

Seeing Is Believing, But Are You Blind?

Try this experiment for the next three days by collecting data that proves each of these two beliefs is true. Keep a simple, written record of the things you see and things you overhear people saying. Be sure to spend some time in a grocery store, in a fast food restaurant, and in a place where lots of kids and parents are gathered for recreation (such as a park, a ball game, or a movie theater).

Belief: Dads are patient, understanding, and enjoy being with their kids.

Data: (examples)

Dad in a grocery store didn't yell at his kid for knocking over the display.

Dad comforted his daughter on the playground when she fell down.

Belief: Moms are impatient, lack understanding, and do not enjoy spending time with their kids.

Data: (examples)

Mom yelling at son in a grocery store because he wanted candy.

Mom annoyed with her daughter who can't make up her mind which sandwich to order.

Overheard one mom telling a sales clerk that she wishes she could have a two-week vacation away from her kids because they're stressing her out.

with their present lives—create a fantasy world by misremembering the past. Their memories and beliefs may barely resemble the truth. Here's why:[26]

- We notice, interpret, and remember people and events in ways that make them fit our initial beliefs and expectations.
- We sometimes remember things very differently from the way they actually happened.
- Many memories are shaped by what others have told us—not by what we actually saw or heard ourselves.
- We tend to forget the bad and remember the good about those people we presently love most.
- We tend to forget the good and remember the bad about people we presently dislike or are angry with.
- The way someone words a question affects what we can and cannot remember.
- How we expect another person to behave in the future is based on how we feel right now.

Now you might be saying to yourself, *Well, even if I can't trust my memories, at least I can trust my feelings.* Well actually, no you can't—at least not without some caution. Even your feelings can be based on some pretty faulty reasoning. When your brain is processing information about what's happening, you are creating a story as you go along. But your story isn't based on objective or complete information. It's based on your existing beliefs, your present mood, and your need to make everything in the present "fit together" neatly with what you think happened in the past. Only *after* you've created your story do you experience a "feeling." For instance, "I'm mad at dad because what he just did means he doesn't like me as

much as he likes my brother" or, "I'm feeling sorry for dad because he's tired and didn't realize it would hurt my feelings
when he did that." Or, "I'm sad because what my daughter just
did means that she doesn't respect me," or "I'm feeling worried
for my daughter because the way she just treated me means
that she's really stressed by her job." So before you put too
much trust in your feelings, remember: Feelings aren't necessarily based on "the truth." Your brain's natural inclination is
to create stories that:

- make you feel good about yourself.
- make the other person look like the jerk or the villain.
- cast the people you like most as good guys and those
  you like least as bad guys.
- interpret things the way you have in the past—even
  when you are wrong.
- make it seem as if what's going on in the present is
  consistent with the past—even in situations where
  this is not true.
- create a unifying theme so you can organize and pre-
  dict events in your life—even when the events were
  not related and not predictable.
- try to convince yourself that there was a cause and effect relationship—even in situations where the events
  were actually random and unrelated.

So Now What?
If you have unpleasant memories that are still limiting or
hurting your relationship, what can you do? First, talk together about those memories. Compare notes. Revisit the
past. See if you can modify or soften some of those hurtful

memories in order to see each other in a better light. Second, take the troublesome memory and ask yourself these questions: How can I get more information about that particular situation? What information might be missing from my version of the story? Is there a more positive way I could interpret that situation now that I'm older? Is there anyone who might have encouraged me to remember that event in such a negative way? Anyone who might have benefited from it?

Consider doing what Jessica did to change the memories and the stories she had been telling herself about her dad. For years she had felt that her dad favored her brother and enjoyed being with him more than with her. The most painful memories were all those times she begged dad to take her camping like he did her brother. To start revisiting the past, she needed to be sure she had her facts right. So she asked her brother and her parents how often her dad took her camping. All three said she was right: There had been no camping trips with dad. But then her mom casually remarked, "When your dad said he wanted to take you camping, I said it wouldn't be right for the two of you to go off alone like that. People might get the wrong impression about a dad and teenage daughter." Whoa! That one new piece of information put a whole new spin on things for Jessica. Dad *had* wanted to take her camping, but mom had vetoed the idea. Then Jessica talked to her dad about those camping trips. To her surprise he said, "You were always so much easier to be around than your brother was. Maybe that's why I was so wiped out after going camping with him. He could be such a pain in the neck when he was a teenager!"

Bingo! Jessica's facts had been correct—*but not complete*—and her interpretation of the facts had been way off base. Her dad's remarks triggered some other memories that she hadn't mixed into the overall picture. She started remembering just how much trouble her brother had been. But she had wrongly assumed that he morphed into "super son" on those camping trips. And she did remember that her dad looked exhausted when he got home from those camping weekends. By believing that her brother was dad's favorite, she interpreted his exhaustion to his having had such a good time camping with super son. In the end, Jessica used the same facts and same memories she had started with, but she was able to change the story she had been telling herself for years about those memories. How about you? Can you follow her lead?

Why Fathers Matter

One of the most destructive beliefs about fathers is that they have less impact on their daughters than mothers do. Another version of this myth is that a daughter won't pay a price later in life for having a distant or a troubled relationship with her father while she's growing up. Carried to the extreme, this means as long as the family has enough money and mom is a good parent, a daughter isn't going to lose out by not having a relationship with her father. Especially if he isn't a "good enough" parent, she's better off without him. Nonsense! Children benefit from being loved—and from knowing that they are loved—by *both* parents, even if one or both of those parents isn't considered "good enough" by other adults' standards. (I'm not referring to those parents who have debilitating, lifelong mental problems that might endanger their children and that prevent them from being able to parent, such as being addicted to drugs, being physically abusive, having a debilitating mental illness, and so forth.)

Contrary to what many seem to believe, dads have a life-long impact on their daughters—as much or more impact than moms. As you can see from the research in the section titled "Your Father, Why Bother?," having a troubled or a distant relationship with her dad while she's growing up leaves an imprint—and seldom a good one—for the rest of a daughter's life. Although the impact usually isn't as negative, a daughter whose father dies early in her life can also pay a price for his absence later in her life. Above all, daughters who haven't grown up with a loving father have a harder time trusting and being emotionally intimate with men. When they marry, these women tend to be overly involved and overly dependent on their children largely because they can't be emotionally intimate with their husbands. And as you can see from the "Boyfriends' Broken Hearts" section on page 37, men who fall in love with these women can also pay a price for her "father issues."

So dads, exactly what effect do you have on your daughters' relationships with men? Aside from you having a tremendous impact on whether or not she becomes pregnant or engages in sexually risky behavior as a teenager, you also influence her choices in men. What types of men does she choose to date? What will she do when she's in a relationship that isn't good for her? Will she be so overly dependent on men that she will do things that aren't in her best interest just to keep her man happy? Here's a brief list of attitudes that you dads want to help your daughters develop:

- I will say how I feel even if I know the man I love will disagree with me.
- Loving someone doesn't mean I always have to put his needs ahead of mine.

- I'm not being selfish to consider my needs as important as those of the man I love.
- I am not going to judge myself solely on the basis of how a man feels about me.
- It is not my responsibility to make a man into a happy person.
- Loving someone doesn't mean I always have to do what makes him happy.
- It's all right to disagree or argue with a man I love.
- I am not going to hide who I am just to make someone love me.
- I am not going to keep trying to change myself to make someone love me.
- It's not selfish to sometimes do things just to please myself.
- It's better to not be in a relationship than to be in one that isn't good for me.
- It's all right to have times in my life when I'm not in a relationship.

This isn't meant to be a comprehensive list of every important attitude that dads instill in their daughters in regard to men. My list is simply intended to highlight the kinds of beliefs that a daughter learns from her dad—beliefs that have a lifelong impact on her relationships with men.

Your Father, Why Bother?

Daughters who had a loving, communicative, active relationship with their dads while they were growing up usually have the advantage over other daughters in these ways:

[35]

- not being overly dependent on men[27]
- not getting pregnant as a teenager [28]
- not abusing drugs or alcohol[29]
- not being arrested[30]
- not developing an eating disorder[31, 32]
- being successful in school and at work[33]
- being able to have intimate, trusting relationships with men[34, 35]
- enjoying and feeling comfortable with her sexuality[36]
- being self-reliant and self-confident[37]
- enjoying good mental health (no clinical depression or anxiety disorders)[38]

An offshoot of the myth that "dad doesn't matter that much" is that he just can't measure up to mom when it comes to raising a daughter. But as you see from the research in the section titled "Father's Report Card" on page 39, a dad's ways of parenting are just as good as a mom's. And by the way, the daughter who "invented" Father's Day realized back in 1909 that a dad's ways of raising kids are just as good as a mom's! True, most fathers and mothers relate differently to their kids and have different opinions about childrearing. But why would we want them to be identical? That's one of the benefits of being raised by two people: They don't always do things the same way. But this doesn't mean that one parent is inferior to the other. We're not doing father-daughter relationships any good, and we're being sexist, when we assume that a dad's ways of parenting are inferior to a mom's just because he's a man.

Father's Day: Bravo for Single Dads!

Who "invented" Father's Day? Sonora Dodd did it in 1909. As a young married woman, Sonora realized what an exceptional father she had. Her father, William Smart, a Civil War veteran, was widowed when his wife died in childbirth with their sixth child. Mr. Smart raised the newborn and the other five kids by himself on a farm in Washington State. Only after she became an adult did Sonora realize how loving and selfless her dad had been. She organized the first Father's Day celebration on June 19, her dad's birthday. In 1924, President Coolidge publicly supported the idea of a national Father's Day, but it wasn't until 1966 that President Johnson officially declared it a national holiday. In 1972, President Nixon signed a law setting the date as the third Sunday of June.

Boyfriends' Broken Hearts: Women with "Father Issues"

"I married a woman whose dad died when she was very young; she left home at the age of fourteen. Several relationships and two kids later, along came me. I can be an excellent caretaker. I asked when we met how she got along with her father. When she told me he was dead, I thought, great, no father issues. How little I knew! We're divorced now, and I am angry at myself. I felt things weren't right, but I married her anyway. There were patterns: always older men, always short, steamy relationships. I feel as if I was both husband and father. It creeps me out. I am going for therapy to try to figure out what my ex wanted or expected from me. I made my mistakes and am trying to learn from them."

[37]

"I am in a relationship with a woman who had a distant father relationship, and I want to get a better understanding of her and her needs. Can you give me some advice in this regard? She's very educated, thirty-five, attractive, funny, generally very upbeat. But she never seems comfortable with any physical contact: hugging, kissing, snuggling, holding hands. She has never had sex with anyone. And I'm not trying to push her into that. She's never been married. Are there issues that I should be sensitive to in this relationship?"

"I feel like a fool because I got myself into such a mess in my marriage. I just didn't see it coming. I knew my wife had never gotten along well with her dad. But since she's got a successful career and seemed like a pretty happy person, it didn't worry me. But soon after we got married, I started seeing another side of her: very critical, very quick to lose her temper, quick to shut down when something was bothering her, very suspicious and jealous. She always thought I was going to cheat on her. The marriage ended because she cheated on me. Now my friends are telling me it probably had something to do with her father issues. What do you think?"

Many daughters do realize, of course, what a wonderful impact their fathers have had on them. Ironically, having a terrific dad can present a problem of a different sort: No other man can measure up to dad. Here's what one young adult daughter wrote to me: "My question concerns not difficult but very *good* relationships between fathers and daughters. In truly healthy, wonderfully communicative, and supportive relationships like mine with my own father, I've found that this kind of "model relationship" with him has almost pushed the bar too high for my other adult relationships with men. I wonder if this is something specific to me."

My advice? There's nothing wrong with comparing other men to your wonderful father. This can help you stay clear of men who aren't good for you or good to you. But it's not good to be overly critical of men your age because they can't measure up to your dad. Remember, these men are much younger than your dad. They have several decades to go before they reach his level of maturity. Also your dad has an advantage over all the other men: He has known you for decades. The men you're dating don't have that advantage. You also want to be sure that you aren't idealizing your dad. You need to see his weaknesses and his imperfections. Can you name several things about him that you don't like? Do you see things he could improve on? Let's hope so. Otherwise, you've got him on a pedestal, and you and the men in your life will always have to look "up" to him. And that's not good.

Father's Report Card

Compared to mothers, fathers are more likely to:[39]
- Challenge the kids intellectually.
- Discourage kids from whining and feeling sorry for themselves.
- Focus on how to solve problems instead of complaining.
- Encourage independence and self-reliance.
- Refuse to give kids too much power over the adults.
- Teach kids to take responsibility for their mistakes.
- Get the kids to try new or difficult things.
- Encourage the kids to try again after failing.
- Motivate kids to reach their full potential.

Daughters' Impact on Their Fathers

When we think about fathers and daughters, chances are most of us think about the ways that he affects her—how he shapes her life; how he influences her opinions; how he creates stress or comfort, or sadness or joy, for her. Dads, let's get the word out: *Daughters have an enormous impact on their fathers as well.* Daughters, you have an impact on your father's opinions, his moods, his self-confidence, his happiness, his stress levels. Your relationship is like a dance. Your moves as a daughter have an impact on your partner—and that partner is your dad. Sometimes a daughter steps on dad's toes; and yes, it does affect him. As a dad, if you've never talked to your daughter about the impact she has on you, now's the time. As a daughter, if you've only been thinking about how your dad affects you, get with the program: Think about how *you* affect *him.*

Another way to appreciate the impact that you, as a daughter, have on your dad is by spending a few hours alone with him talking about these questions:

- What has been fun about being a father?
- How has being a father changed you?
- As a young father, what worried you and what pleased you the most?
- What has surprised you about yourself as a parent?
- What have some of your most stressful times been as a dad?
- How has having kids affected your personality?
- How is having a daughter different from having a son in terms of its impact on you?
- How have you changed over the years as a father?
- What were some of the hardest changes for you to make as a parent?

Father-Daughter Dance: A Daughter's Impact

Male congressmen who have daughters are more likely to support women's issues than congressmen without daughters. Those with daughters are more likely to vote for bills on reproductive rights, women's safety, equal opportunities in the workforce, and educational equity. Yale researchers found this to be true on more than twenty women's issues in Congress from 1997 to 2004.[40]

William Shakespeare left most of his estate to his eldest daughter Suzanna, not to his wife. Three of his final plays are centered on father-daughter relationships. At the end of his life he moved back to Stratford, perhaps to live near his daughter, her husband, and their child.[41]

President John Adams (1735–1826), who helped write the Declaration of Independence, developed a deep friendship with his daughter Nabby. Their letters reveal that she was one of his closest political advisors. She served as his sounding board during his times of trouble and fame as president of the United States.[42]

Fred Ruiz is the CEO of Ruiz Foods in Dinuba, California, which produces frozen Mexican food and distributes it nationwide. He says his oldest daughter, Kim Ruiz Beck, helped modernize his thinking about women in the business world. He thought the male-dominated business environment was not a place for women. "When she got her bachelor's and master's degrees, it made it easier for me to change my attitudes and my perspectives in regard to women in the workplace and their abilities to perform and be responsible."[43]

Jeffrey Runge is the chief medical officer for the Department of Homeland Security. When he was heading up the National Highway Traffic Safety Administration, he asked his college student daughter for advice on how to market safe driving ideas to young people. "She gave me terrific advice on the lack of effectiveness of some of our drunk driving messages."[44]

- What are some of the best gifts or compliments I've ever given you?
- How have you changed since you first became a dad?
- What impact have I had on your life?
- How have I influenced any of your opinions or your decisions in life?

African American Fathers

If you're African American, have you ever felt that your wonderful father-daughter relationship is overshadowed by all of the negative messages about black fathers in our country? Many "top pops" are ignored in the media—black dads who have never been in jail, have been good parents and husbands, and earn decent incomes. If you're one of these dads, you rarely get public attention. Decent black dads don't make the headlines, but they are certainly out there. They quietly support their families, raise their kids, and take care of their elderly parents. And the impact on their daughters is profound.

Unfortunately, black fathers are up against some very negative stereotypes in the media. Even today most movies and music videos still show African American men as thugs, criminals, or out-of-control athletes.[45-47] In many popular novels and movies, such as *How Stella Got Her Groove Back* or *Waiting to Exhale*, the men are a sorry bunch. Rarely is there a documentary like *Diary of a Tired Black Man* in which the black man's feelings and experiences with women are presented in a compassionate way.[48] No wonder movies like *Pursuit of Happyness* or *Daddies Girls* catch our attention. Finally, the black father is the hero, not the villain. With so many negative messages about African American dads floating around in our society, it's especially important to spread the good news: Millions of these dads are doing a fine job raising their daughters.[49-51]

Daughters with Loving Dads[52]

Beyoncé Knowles, award-winning singer and actress

"What I love most about my father is his ability to love his family so effortlessly, so completely. Basically my father taught me what it means to be loved by a man and respected by a man. And I have carried that with me my entire life."

Leah Sears, chief justice, Georgia Supreme Court

"I think my father was most proud of me when I called and told him I'd passed the bar. He simply said, 'Okay, pretty baby. Good.' I mean, Okay, pretty baby? Tell me! Say something! But my mother told me months after that he couldn't sleep the whole night. He paced the floor the whole night saying, 'My daughter's a lawyer. My daughter's a lawyer. I can't believe it!'"

Alana Beard, All-Star, Women's National Basketball Association

"My father is a truck driver. His job is dangerous because he hauls chemicals, but he's done it for twenty-three years, and it's something that I've always admired about him. As much as he stayed on the road during the week, he always made time for us on the weekends. Whether that would be taking us out to eat or taking us to the park to play basketball with our friends. He was there."

Deborah Roberts, national correspondent, ABC news

"Toward the end of his life I felt very close to my father, and it was very important for me to try to build upon the relationship that we had. I'm grateful that I had the opportunity.

I can say that I have seen the complete picture of my fa-
ther—the man he had been and the man he eventually be-
came."

Rasham Ali, host of the top-rated *A Team Morning*
Show in Atlanta

Girls need so much from their dads—from love to en-
couragement to that silent time that I love so much. A man
to show you how to pick yourself up, to teach you how to
ride your bike, to show you what to look for in a man. I love
the way he loves me.

Internet Resources

Let's continue to replace negative beliefs and half-truths with
facts and research. One way to do this is to head for the Web.
The Internet offers dozens of Web sites rich with resources for
dads and daughters. Each of the sites listed in "Internet Resources" box on the page 46 is sponsored by a respected national organization or by professionals who are experts in their
field. Visit these Web sites regularly. Talk to each other about
what you find there. Share the information with other dads
and daughters. Free yourself from blinding, binding beliefs and
help other fathers and daughters do the same.

Black Fathers: Speaking About Fatherhood

Ruffin: "I have an eternal bond with my children. They will always be my daughters, and I will be their father. If they will remember me as Papa, a man who gave of himself, I will be satisfied that it has been worth the struggle."[53]

Stubblefield: "I'm trying to work on bringing us back together as a family. I had to come to grips with myself on the fact that we don't build relationships overnight. It goes back to trust. You just have to learn to trust each other. There are still some rough turns on the right path, but I just ask God to give me strength."[54]

Noel: "As black men we are often conditioned by the negative images of us, about what we lack, about what we fail to do, about how we are missing from our family as fathers. Yet the image of fatherhood, even in white society, is simplified to one of financial provider, which can still make you feel inadequate sometimes. What I am learning more and more is that providing may not be providing much—that my attentive presence, my hugs, and my time are all that my child really wants from me, and that makes me feel free."[55]

Jeff: "A pop is a teacher. A pop is sensitive. A pop is loving. A pop shows you the steps. A pop corrects you. A pop gives you direction. I am blessed to be a pop. I was never blessed with a pop."[56]

Charles: "In March of this year my youngest daughter presented us with a grandson. As I stood in the hospital holding him, I realized that I was the first man in my family ever to hold his first-born grandson. The ravages of war, crime, separation, disease, and early death had denied our family that sign of continuity. The revelation made me cry."[57]

Internet Resources

Fatherhood
Dads and Daughters - dadsanddaughters.org
Fathers Direct - fathersdirect.com
National Fatherhood Initiative - fatherhood.org
Stay at Home Dads - slowlane.com

Divorced or Single Fathers
American Coalition for Fathers & Children - acfc.org
Divorced Fathers Network - divorcedfathers.com
Fathers for Justice - fathers-4-justice.com
Fathers and Families - ncfc.org
Fathers in Touch - fathersintouch.org
National Fathers Resource Center - fathers4kids.org
Children's Rights Council - crc.org

Documentaries
Daddy Hunger by Ray Upchurch - daddyhunger.com
Papa Was a Rolling Stone by Robin Wright King -
    robinwrightking.com
Diary of a Tired Black Man by Tim Alexander -
    tiredblackman.com
The Evolution of Dad - evolutionofdad.com

African American Dads
African American Coalition for Shared Parenting - acfc.org
Black Men Raising Girls Alone - bmrga.com
Children Need Both Parents - cnppinc.org
Fathers in Touch - fathersintouch.org
Proud Poppa - proudpoppa.net

Communicating: We Can Do Better Than This ❖ 3

- *Why is it so hard for us to communicate?*
- *Why does my daughter get so upset when I try to give her advice?*
- *Why is my dad always criticizing me or telling me how to run my life?*
- *Why does my daughter accuse me of not listening to her?*
- *Why does my dad seem so distant when I try to talk to him?*
- *Why can't we talk comfortably or honestly about personal things?*
- *Why is it so hard for us to talk to each other when it's just the two of us?*
- *Is it too late to improve our communication at this point in our lives?*
- *How do we know which upsetting things from the past we should still talk about and which ones we should just let go?*
- *Why does my daughter cry or walk out on me instead of talking things out?*
- *Why can't dad talk to me like a grown-up instead of like a little girl?*

Sound familiar? In this chapter we'll be answering questions like these. But you might already be asking yourself: "What if only one of us wants to change the way we communicate? Don't both of us have to work on this together if it is going to improve? Don't we both have to admit that we are each partly at fault for our communication problems?" Let's face it; most of us think we communicate better than other people do. We waste a lot of energy focusing on the other person's flaws rather than our own. So as you read this chapter, take a different approach: Focus only on the improvements that *you* can make in communicating. Changing the way you communicate is a gift you give yourself because you're going to feel more relaxed and more satisfied with yourself even if the other person doesn't change.

Your Emotional Intelligence

Let's start by using the following quiz to figure out how you two typically communicate with each other.

The behaviors noted in the quiz are called "emotional intelligence."[1] Emotional intelligence means being able to talk comfortably about personal, emotional things; to sense what others are feeling; to be aware of your own feelings; to listen attentively; to initiate conversations and keep them going; and to express your emotions in ways that don't damage your relationships. When it comes to emotional intelligence, how smart or how dumb we are usually depends on who we are interacting with—and what the situation is. For example, you might give yourself a great score on the quiz if you're rating the way you interact with your co-workers, your neighbors, or your best friend. But, as father and daughter, you might give yourselves much lower scores when it comes to the way you interact with each other. Wouldn't it be great if our emotional intelli-

How Emotionally Intelligent Are You?

How do you generally communicate with each other? Each of you should fill out the dad and the daughter columns so that you can compare your answers.

0 = never   1 = rarely   2 = usually   3 = almost always

Dad   Daughter

_____ _____ Expresses feelings openly and comfortably.

_____ _____ Recognizes what the other person is feeling.

_____ _____ Expresses anger in an appropriate way.

_____ _____ Shows sympathy and concern for the other.

_____ _____ Handles conflicts or disagreements by talking about them.

_____ _____ Feels comfortable when the other person expresses feelings.

_____ _____ Lets the other person finish what they're saying without interrupting.

_____ _____ States opinions without insulting the other person.

_____ _____ Pays attention while the other is talking.

_____ _____ Interprets nonverbal messages accurately.

_____ _____ Maintains eye contact and looks relaxed when you're talking to each other.

_____ _____ Accepts negative feedback without getting angry or defensive.

_____ _____ Expresses emotions without becoming overwhelmed by them.

_____ _____ Draws people into conversations and makes them feel comfortable.

_____ _____ Discusses controversial topics without insulting the other person.

_____ _____ **Your scores** (45 possible)

gence always functioned at its best when we're with the people we love most—or when we're dealing with those issues that mean the most to us? Unfortunately it doesn't. Our emotional intelligence too often deserts us just when we need it most.

So if we're only rating how each of you behave in your father-daughter interactions, how emotionally intelligent are you? Where do each of you need to improve? If you scored above forty, you're very emotionally intelligent when you're interacting with each other. You have great communication skills. But if you scored below twenty, you've got a lot of new skills to learn. The lower your score, the more likely you are to hear comments such as:

"You're not listening to me."

"You don't understand how I feel."

"You're so distant and hard to get to know."

"Why can't you tell me how you feel without getting angry or clamming up?"

Many adult daughters are more emotionally or more socially intelligent than their fathers.[2-3] Is this because men aren't interested in communicating? No. Is it because women are by nature better communicators than men? No. Is it because men are less sensitive or less understanding than women or that men don't have as many feelings as women do? No.

Then what's going on? Just this—little girls are generally taught more emotional or social communication skills than little boys.[4] These skills are learned, not inborn. For example, when little boys feel afraid or someone hurts their feelings, they are usually taught not to express feelings. Not wanting to be called "sissies," little boys learn to hide feelings of fear, loneliness, insecurity, or pain. Don't cry. Don't talk about your feelings. And don't talk about personal things. Talk sports or school or television or movies. But don't talk personal stuff the way girls do. Given how differently most males and females have been taught to communicate, it's no surprise that many fathers score lower than their daughters on an emotional intelligence test.

So as father and daughter, first recognize that you communicate differently largely because this is what each of you has been taught to do. Second, recognize that no matter how old you are, you can raise your emotional intelligence by learning new skills. For example, as a dad you can learn to turn off the television or put down the paper when your daughter is trying to talk to you so that she won't accuse you of not listening to her. Spend less time asking her for the facts ("What's new lately?") and more time asking about her feelings ("Tell me about what made you happiest or saddest lately.")—that's emotional intelligence. As a daughter you can learn not to start important conversations with your father when he is pre-occupied or physically exhausted. For instance, don't start a serious conversation as soon as he gets home from work or when he's at his wits' end trying to fix a leaky faucet. When you stop pouting or walking away when you're frustrated with him—that's emotional intelligence.

Emotional intelligence also means being able to correctly interpret what the other person is feeling. For example, when dad keeps watching television while his daughter is trying to talk to him, she gets angry because she interprets this to mean: "He isn't interested in what's going on in my life." Meanwhile, dad feels disappointed and misunderstood because he interprets his daughter's anger to mean: "If she had any consideration for how hard I work, she'd know by now that watching television when I first get home is the only way I can relax." So who's at fault—father or daughter? The answer is neither. Both lack certain emotional intelligence skills, and both are making assumptions that are hurting their relationship.

See if you can figure out what's going on between this father and daughter based on their comments:

> **Amy:** *"I love my dad but it's hard to talk to him; he just isn't very sensitive or in touch with his feelings. It's like nothing gets to him emotionally. Can you believe that I have never seen him cry—not even at his mother's funeral? Of course I don't talk to him about emotional or personal things because he isn't sensitive enough to understand what I'm going through. Besides, he isn't interested in what's going on in my life. He never—and I mean never—asks me anything about my friends or my boyfriend. He just doesn't seem to care about anything except how I'm doing in school or with my part-time job. The way we communicate is just fine with him. That's just the kind of guy he is."*

> **Jake:** *"I really love my daughter but she just doesn't want me to know anything about her life other than school or work. It's like she's pushing me away. She never talks to me about her friends or her boyfriend. I'm afraid to bring these things up because she'd probably snap my head off and say I was prying into her personal life. To be honest, it hurts my feelings the way she shuts me out. Actually, sometimes she treats me like I don't have any feelings. I mean, at my mother's funeral when I had to leave the room a couple of times to stop from falling apart in front of everyone, Amy actually seemed aggravated with me. Now what was that all about?"*

Are Men Blockheads?

The way dads and daughters communicate is also affected by what both of you believe about how well men communicate compared to women. Remember what you learned from chapter two: Whatever you believe is true about a particular group of people has a profound impact on how you treat anyone who happens to be a member of that group—even when your beliefs are not accurate. For example, if you believe that men are "communication blockheads" compared to women, then that belief can interfere with your father-daughter relationship. So use the quiz on the next page to see how accurate your beliefs are and to see which of your beliefs may be limiting your relationship.

What was your score? Hopefully, zero. None of these negative beliefs are true for most men in our country today. Sure, some men behave in these ways, just like some women do. But most men don't. For the sake of your father-daughter relationship, you need to let go of any potentially damaging beliefs you have about men.

Speak Up, Dads!

Daughters who communicate well with their fathers are less likely to develop eating disorders.[5]

Daughters whose fathers talk with them about sex and dating are less likely to get pregnant as teenagers, to catch a sexually transmitted disease, or to have sex as young teenagers.[6,7]

The teenage daughter, not the dad, is often the one who doesn't want to talk about sex or dating.[8-10]

Most adult daughters wish they had spent more time talking to their fathers while they were growing up rather than having ignored or pushed them away.[11-13]

Are Men Blockheads?

Dad and daughters, which statements do you believe are true for most men in our country?

Score 1 point for each question you answer true.

Dad Daughter

_____ _____ Men talk much more about themselves than women do.

_____ _____ Men express anger more often than women do.

_____ _____ Men do much more of the talking than women do.

_____ _____ Men dominate most conversations while women tend to listen.

_____ _____ Men interrupt more than women do.

_____ _____ Men have an easier time letting others know when their feelings are hurt.

_____ _____ Men can deal with women's anger easier than women can deal with men's.

_____ _____ Men become angry faster and stay angry longer than women do.

_____ _____ Men criticize and ridicule people more than women do.

_____ _____ Men are less sympathetic and less compassionate than women.

_____ _____ **Score** (10 possible)

Feeling Less Afraid

Why is it that the more important a conversation is with someone we love, the more likely we are to mess it up? Why do we usually say and do the most hurtful and stupid things in our "crucial" conversations? In part it's because we feel vulnerable and afraid—afraid that the relationship is going to be worse off if we speak honestly or share our true feelings. When we feel vulnerable or afraid, we communicate at our worst. So use this "Your Crucial Conversations" checklist to see what each of you do that makes the other vulnerable or afraid.[14] The higher your scores, the more difficult it is for the two of you to have a crucial conversation. Read the quiz on page 57 for ways to improve your crucial conversations.

Remember that the goal is to help each other feel comfortable enough to talk honestly and openly. This can only happen when you understand what you and the other person are afraid might happen in an honest conversation. So before you start a crucial conversation, ask yourself these questions: What are we each afraid might happen if we talk honestly and openly? What can each of us do to put each other at ease?

Take a look at this father-daughter situation. What could each of them do before they start their conversation to put each other more at ease?

Ethan: *"My daughter keeps asking me for money even though she has graduated from college and has a job. I love Jada, but she's old enough now to handle her own financial problems. I'm afraid that if I say no to her she'll refuse to come to the family reunion next month. That's what she did a few years ago when she got mad at me. I'm also afraid she'll storm out of the room in tears like she usually does when I don't give her what she wants. It's probably*

Your Crucial Conversations

How do you each generally behave when you're having a "crucial" conversation?

0 = never   1 = rarely   2 = usually   3 = almost always

Father Daughter

_____ _____ Clam up

_____ _____ Only give short answers

_____ _____ Joke or laugh at a serious comment

_____ _____ Make insulting or sarcastic remarks

_____ _____ Walk away

_____ _____ Hang up

_____ _____ Change the subject

_____ _____ Exaggerate in order to make a point

_____ _____ Yell or curse

_____ _____ Sidestep or avoid questions

_____ _____ Look or sound bored or uninterested

_____ _____ Name call

_____ _____ Cry or pout

_____ _____ Make "all or nothing" comments (never, always, everyone)

_____ _____ Label each other ("you men," "you college kids")

_____ _____ Deny that you are upset when you are

_____ _____ Interrupt a lot

_____ _____ Talk louder or faster

_____ _____ Attack the other's intelligence

_____ _____ Act as if the topic is trivial or unimportant

_____ _____ **Your scores** (60 possible)

[56]

Improving Your Conversations

Which of these do you, as a father or daughter, do in your crucial conversations?

_____ Talk in private so that nobody else can interfere or interrupt.

_____ Talk when neither of us is tired, grumpy, or preoccupied.

_____ Encourage each other to keep talking. ("Tell me more." "And what else?")

_____ Find things that you agree on and state them, such as "I'm glad we both agree that . . ."

_____ Use the word *and* instead of *but* as often as you can.

_____ Find a shared goal and state it. ("We both want to find a good solution for this.")

_____ Reassure each other that you're not out to hurt, punish, blame, or humiliate the other person.

_____ Don't state your opinions as if they were facts.

_____ Compliment each other for something.

_____ Avoid judgmental words. ("How stupid!")

_____ **Your score** (10 possible)

easier just to give her the money. But I really feel bad doing that. It's treating her like a baby. My neck starts to tense up just thinking about having to talk to her about this."

Jada: "I dread talking to Pops about money again. But my credit card is maxed out. Whenever I ask him for money, he raises his voice and starts pacing, like he's really going to explode. And he's got this vein on the side of his forehead that starts to bulge when he's getting upset with me. Then he starts lecturing me about how I need to grow up and how irresponsible I am. I'm just going to have mom get the money from him so he can't hassle me."

Not Fair!

- Comic strips, greeting cards, television shows, and movies portray fathers as far more incompetent and insensitive than mothers in communicating with their kids.[15-19]
- Men are rarely allowed to express sadness by crying in movies or on television.[20]

Advice or Interference?

The most common complaint I hear from daughters of every age is: "My dad is always trying to tell me how to run my life—always criticizing me. He treats me like a child. He needs to trust my judgment instead of giving me advice. I just want him to understand my feelings." And from dads what I usually hear is something like this: "Whenever I try to help my daughter, she snaps my head off and accuses me of trying to run her life. I want to save her from making the same mistakes I made when I was her age. I love her so much that I don't want her to go through what I went through. But when I try to give her advice she either clams up or explodes. It's like she wants me to listen to her complain and watch her suffer without doing anything." What's going on here? Why do so many fathers and daughters end up hurt or frustrated when dad is trying to give advice? Generally speaking, there are four pieces to this puzzle.

1) Empathize, then advise. Unlike boys, girls are usually taught to talk about how the other person is feeling before offering any advice. They show this empathy by saying things such as:

"I know just how you feel. Something like that happened to me once and it was awful."

"You must have felt so embarrassed when that happened."

"I bet you're heartbroken, aren't you?"

Most women have been taught to gently offer advice in a carefully worded, tentative way such as:

"Do you think it might help if . . . ,"

"One thing I did when I was in a similar situation like yours was . . ."

"I'm not sure this would work, but you might want to . . ."

In contrast, most males have been taught to jump right in and offer advice on how to fix whatever is wrong, whether it's a broken heart or a broken car. Because a loving father can't bear to see his daughter unhappy, he tries to ease her pain by offering solutions to whatever is upsetting her. He's not an insensitive idiot who doesn't understand how she feels. After all, he's probably been through similar situations himself. But why dwell on the feelings of misery? What good does that do? Let's get on with putting an end to her pain. So a dad does

[59]

what he has been trained to do—rescue his daughter from her pain as quickly as he can.

2) Blunt nurturance. Most men have been taught to communicate more bluntly and more directly than women. While many of us find this refreshing, daughters often find it upsetting. For instance, dad might say, "Your boyfriend sure bosses you around a lot." While mom might say, "Have you ever wondered if you ought to speak up for yourself a little more with your boyfriend?" Both parents are being nurturing. But odds are that dad's blunt, direct style is going to upset his daughter unless she learns to recognize the tender motives behind his blunt words. Dads, be a little less brusque so your daughters have an easier time seeing your nurturing, protective motives.

3) Who is judging you? When someone gives us advice, we often tell ourselves, "She thinks I'm an idiot. He's ashamed of me. I'm a failure." In fact, the harshest judgment and criticism are usually coming from you, not the other person. That nagging, critical voice that's saying *"you screwed up"* or *"you're an idiot"* is yours, not the other person's. In your father-daughter relationship it's usually dad who is giving the advice because he's got more experience and because one of the unpleasant responsibilities of being a loving parent is to advise your kids. As a dad, remember that your daughter—no matter how old she is—may still be trying to prove to you that she's an intelligent, mature person. So when you're giving her advice, she's thinking, "How am I going to prove to dad that I'm not an idiot?"

As a daughter, why not let your dad know that you need a little reassurance along with his advice? You might say something like:

"I'm getting the feeling that you think I'm immature and irre-

sponsible. It sure would help right now if you'd let me know that you think I generally do a pretty good job in handling things."

"I'm feeling like you're really ashamed of me, that I'm a huge embarrassment to you. Am I?"

When daughters do this, they're usually surprised to hear their fathers say such things as:

"I'm not mad at you. I'm just scared. I'm scared that worse things will happen to you if you don't follow some of my advice."

"Of course I don't think you're stupid. It's just that I learned the hard way about this sort of thing, and I don't want to see you get hurt the way I did."

4) Perfect daddy. As a father, you don't want your daughter to think of you as her "perfect daddy" by the time she reaches adulthood. Why? Because if she still has you on a pedestal, it's harder for her to accept advice from you; after all, you're Mr. Perfect who never made any of the mistakes she makes. Mr. Perfect never needed advice and guidance from his father. Mr. Perfect never ignored his father's advice the way she sometimes ignores yours. It's hard to accept advice from someone we think is superior to us—superior because they don't make the same kinds of mistakes we make. Trust me on this one. Your daughter will feel more comfortable accepting advice and coming to you for help when you let her know that you're not her moral superior and that you've made plenty of mistakes along the way.

As a daughter, you will feel more comfortable listening to your dad's advice if you see him as a human being who makes mistakes just like you do. So when you go to your dad for advice, first ask him to tell you about his own blunders. "Dad, I'd like to know if you've ever been in a situation like the one I'm going to tell you about. Before you give me any advice, I'd like to hear what happened to you, and how you felt at the time.

Who did you go to for advice and did you follow it? How did you feel when your dad gave you advice?"

When a daughter is telling her father about an upsetting situation, the odds are she wants his sympathy, not his advice. Unfortunately, dad may not realize this. He sees his daughter in distress, and because he loves her, he starts trying to "fix it." Much to his surprise, his daughter often gets even more upset. "You're not being sympathetic. You don't understand how I feel. Stop telling me what to do." So what's a father to do? How can a daughter get what she needs from her well-meaning dad?

Daughters, before you tell your father what you're upset about, tell him whether you want his sympathy or his advice. It's your responsibility to let him know what you want—and to figure that out for yourself before you go to him. Do you want sympathy, a dad who simply listens and comforts? "You poor thing. I feel so bad for you." Or do you want his advice, a dad who gives you his ideas on how to improve or fix things? Maybe you want a combination, first his sympathy, then his advice. "Dad, I'm really upset, and I want to tell you about it. But I'm too upset right now to talk about ways to fix things. I just need your shoulder to cry on. When I'm ready, I'll be back for advice."

And daughters, don't tell your dad you want his advice, then get mad at him when he gives it. That's entrapment and that's not fair. There's no way to give other people advice without pointing out where they went wrong and offering a better way of doing things. So if you're not willing to let your dad do that, tell him you don't want his advice—at least not yet.

Fathers, before you start to give advice, ask your daughter, "Do you really want my honest feedback or do you just need a shoulder to cry on?" Be direct. Ask her a second time, just to be sure you got it right. "So what you want from me right now is just to listen—not to help you fix things, right?" or, "So do you want me to give you ideas about how to make this better?"

As a daughter ages, there are more situations where she is in a position to offer advice to her father. The same rules apply; ask your father if he wants advice or sympathy, or the "combo."

Let's consider Lynn and her dad Scott. Where do you think they're going wrong and what can they do about it?

> **Lynn:** *"No wonder I don't go to dad for advice. When I told him about the problem I'm having with my boyfriend, he immediately started telling me what to do. I mean, my eyes are still swollen and red from crying. But he's so insensitive that he just starts some big lecture on what I should do. Can't he see how much pain I'm in? Hasn't he ever been heartbroken before?"*

> **Scott:** *"I just can't win. My daughter was telling me yesterday about the trouble she and her boyfriend are having. She was all upset and crying. That really gets to me when I see her in pain like that. So I started telling her what she could do to straighten things out. And she storms out of the room saying that I don't understand how she feels. Today she is still mad at me. What's going on with her?"*

QUIZ

Volcanoes: Handling Anger

When you are angry with each other, how do you usually treat each other?

0 = never 1 = rarely 2 = usually 3 = almost always

Father Daughter

_____ _____ Clam up or refuses to talk any more about it

_____ _____ Pout

_____ _____ Yell

_____ _____ Leave the room or hang up

_____ _____ Drink too much

_____ _____ Turn on music or television for distraction

_____ _____ Withdraw emotionally (the silent treatment, the cold shoulder)

_____ _____ Curse

_____ _____ Say mean things

_____ _____ Cry or try to get your pity

_____ _____ Complain to someone else instead of working it out together

_____ _____ Threaten to do something that would hurt the other emotionally

_____ _____ **Your scores** (36 possible)

Dad's Candor [21, 22]

- Fathers are usually more direct and blunt than mothers when talking to their kids.
- Fathers are more likely than mothers to offer advice on how to fix problems instead of just talking about how bad the child feels.
- Fathers are less likely than mothers to let children whine, complain, or feel sorry for themselves.

Dealing with Anger

Use the quiz on the opposite page to see how you two behave when you're angry with each other. Remember: Your goal is to change *your* behavior, not the other person's. The higher your score, the more you need to change your ways of dealing with anger.

Don't be a backstabber. Don't go to other family members to express your anger or try to get them to take your side. Whatever is making you angry, express it face to face. And don't drag other family members into it. Put yourself in the other person's place. How do you feel when someone goes behind your back instead of telling you why they're upset with you? It hurts, right? Or it makes you mad. And how do you feel when someone tries to get others to take their side against you? Don't you feel ganged up on?

Name your fear. Do you bottle up your anger inside and let it fester? If you do, that's probably happening because you're afraid that expressing your anger is somehow going to make things worse. But worse in what way? What is it you fear might happen? Are you afraid your daughter will love you less if you tell her you're angry about the things she said to you yesterday? Or are you afraid your father will refuse to visit you and your new husband if you tell him how mad you are at him for what he did at the Thanksgiving dinner? Or are you afraid the person will drink too much if you tell him or her you're mad at them? It usually helps to get your fear out in the open, to tell the other person what you're afraid of. (The exception is when either person has been physically violent in the past.)

Your anger histories. Dad usually knows why his daughter deals with anger the way she does because he's been in her life since she was born. But she's often clueless about her father's "anger history." How did he learn to handle anger when he was growing up? What experiences with anger did he have as a young person? How have those experiences shaped the way he deals with anger now? Having this information can help a daughter be more compassionate and sympathetic if the father handles anger in unhealthy ways. The same is true for the father who wasn't part of his daughter's life when she was growing up because he wasn't living with her mother. This dad can benefit from asking his daughter about her anger history. When you're both relaxed and alone with each other, talk about the questions in the "Your Anger History" box.

Emotional Blackmail

Have you ever left a conversation feeling that you were somehow tricked into doing something you really didn't want to do? Do you wonder how the other person managed to manipulate you? In many cases you've been the victim of a manipulative style of communicating referred to as "emotional blackmail."[23] Emotional blackmailers threaten to deprive you of those things they know you want the most. They get you to

Your Anger History

- When you were growing up, how did you let people know you were angry?
- What impact did your anger have on other people?
- What worried you the most when you let others know that you were angry?
- How did people in your family deal with anger?
- When the person got angry at you, how did it affect you?
- What's the best way for people to let you know that they're mad at you?
- What's the hardest for you when someone is mad at you?
- What's hard for you in expressing your anger?
- What lessons have you learned about getting angry or dealing with others' anger?

do what they want by surrounding you with FOG: Fear, Obligation, and Guilt. They try to make you feel afraid by threatening to withdraw something they control—love, approval, money. They make you feel obligated as though you owe them something in return for whatever they have done for you. They try to make you feel guilty. Here are a few FOG statements:

"How could you refuse to do this for me after all I've done for you?"

"I wouldn't feel so depressed if you were willing to . . ."

"You're so selfish and disloyal."

The best emotional blackmailers make it nearly impossible to recognize what they're doing, while they're doing it. It may take days or even years before you realize how the blackmailer manipulates you. Why? In part because when we give blackmailers what they want, they give us goodies—love, praise, approval, attention, promotion, gifts, money—and that feels good. Many emotional blackmailers come across as weak, powerless, and fragile so we end up feeling sorry for them. And once we feel sorry for them, we don't see how much power they have had manipulating us into doing what they wanted.

So how can father or daughter deal with emotional blackmail? First, the person being blackmailed needs to step back and assess the situation: Exactly what is it she/he wants me to do? What emotional weapons is this person using: fear, obligation, or guilt? What usually happens if I don't cave in? Does the person cry, yell, withdraw, give me "the look," or threaten to take something away from me? What is he or she trying to make me feel: afraid, guilty, selfish, disloyal, ungrateful? What belief of mine makes it so easy for this person to keep on blackmailing me? Do I believe it's my duty to always make this person happy? Do I believe love means always giving the other person what he or she wants?

Second, tell the other person how they're blackmailing you and how it makes you feel. For example, a blackmailed father might say: "You're trying to get me to do what you want by crying and by giving me the cold shoulder afterward. That makes me feel manipulated. And it hurts me when you say that I'm selfish just because I won't agree to do what you want me to do." Or a blackmailed daughter might say: "I'm angry because you're trying to get me to do things your way by using religion to make me feel guilty" or "I'm hurt because you seem to be bribing me with money to get me to give in to you on this."

Third, bring the conversation to an end once it's clear that there isn't going to be any compromise or any agreement on this issue. After you've each explained what you want and how you feel, if you're getting nowhere, one of you needs to bring the conversation to an end. Here are a few good ways to end the battle:

"I feel bad that you're still mad at me and that we can't find a solution or a compromise. I do understand your point of view and how you feel. But I'm not going to do what you're asking. So let's call it quits now."

"In the past I have been so hurt when you accuse me of being selfish that I have given in to you even when it goes against what I believe in. But I'm not going to continue that pattern. It's not good for me. Let's just give this a rest now."

"I know you're hurt; but I can't do something that I don't believe in just to make you happy. And this situation isn't something I can compromise on."

"I know you're really disappointed with my decision. But our relationship is too important to let this come between us."

Asking for Change

As father and daughter there are times when you want the other person to change. Remember: You can't "make" the other person change. That is his or her decision. All you can do is learn how to ask for change in a way that does the least damage to your relationship. Try this three-step method:

1) Feeling first. Start out by saying what you feel when the other person does "that"—that thing you want him or her to change. Don't start out by asking the other person to change.

Start with your feeling. Stating your feeling helps the other person understand *why* you're asking for a change and how negative an impact their behavior is having on your relationship. A feeling can't be right or wrong; it's simply a feeling. For example, you could start with: "I feel sad when all you talk about with me is my job." Or, "It makes me feel unloved when you always tell your mom your important news and then she has to tell me." Or, "I feel sad that we seem to be drifting apart because we never spend time together, just the two of us, anymore."

2) *Only ask for* one *change*. Don't ask for a major over-haul—just a little tune-up. Don't reel off a big list of all the things you want the other person to change about himself or herself. Just focus on the one change you think would make the biggest improvement in your relationship. For example, Sally is asking for a major overhaul when she says to her dad: "If you would only change your lifestyle and your attitudes about women, our relationship would be great." Instead, she should ask for a tune-up: "Dad, I'd like you to stop making so many negative comments about women in front of me."

3) *Be specific*. When we ask people to change something about themselves, we tend to use words that are vague and confusing—words that might mean one thing to you and something else to the other person—words that don't make clear exactly what you want the other person to do differently. For instance, if you say, "I want you to pay more attention to me," you might really mean, "I want you to look at me when I'm talking to you" or you might mean, "I want you to ask me more questions about what's going on in my life." If you say, "Stop embarrassing me," you might mean, "Don't curse around my friends," or "Don't drink too much at restaurants," or

"Don't wear that awful shirt again in public with me." So instead of saying, "I want you to show me more respect," a dad should say to his daughter: "I want you to stop using curse words and calling me names when we're arguing with each other." When you combine your feeling with a specific request, it will sound like this: "I'd feel closer to you if you would ask me more questions about things other than my work." "I'd like it a lot if every now and then you'd tell me things before you tell your mom." "Would you be willing to spend one Sunday afternoon a month just with me, just the two of us hanging out together?"

Asking for Change: What Exactly Do You Want?

Reword these statements in a more specific, precise way.

"You need to listen more carefully to me."

"Stop treating me like a child."

"Don't be so condescending and insulting."

"I want you to respect my opinions."

"Don't put me on a guilt trip."

"Don't embarrass me."

"Why do you have to be so uptight?"

"I want you to trust me."

"Stop trying to run my life."

Accepting Me for Myself

When you think about fathers and daughters, which of them pops into your head first when you hear comments such as these: "I just wish I could be accepted for who I am." "Sometimes I feel like I'm not measuring up to what's expected of me." "I wish I could just be myself and not worry about being

[71]

rejected or criticized." "I'm under pressure to be someone that I'm not—like I'm never quite good enough or not quite lovable enough when I'm just being me." "There are times I have to pretend to be someone other than who I really am because I wouldn't be loved or respected as much if I was just myself." "Sometimes I feel like a phony—an imposter who says or does whatever it takes to get the love and acceptance I want." "When I'm hiding the real me, I feel a little sad, a little guilty, and a little lonely."

Most of us probably think of daughters when we hear comments like these. We assume that when it comes to feeling accepted and loved for "just being myself," dads don't feel this way—only daughters do. How ridiculous! A dad can feel just as insecure and just as vulnerable as his daughter when it comes to feeling loved and appreciated for who he really is. A dad can feel—or fear—that he isn't living up to his daughter's expectations. He can feel—and fear—that she's comparing him to other dads and that he isn't stacking up too well. He can feel—and fear—that he can't always be himself around his daughter because she will mock him, or criticize him, or reject him, or think less of him. He can feel just as tense and just as insecure as she does in situations where he's worried that his comments or his behavior will disappoint or anger her. In other words, an adult daughter needs to realize that her dad wants acceptance and approval just as much as she does—no matter how old he is, or how rich he is, or how confident and successful he is outside the family.

As father and daughter, talking candidly together about acceptance and approval can help both of you feel freer to be yourselves around each other. Dads, you need to put yourself out there. Tell your daughter which of her expectations are hardest for you to live up to. Tell her about the ways in which she doesn't seem willing to let you be yourself—or to accept you for who you are. Daughters, stop thinking of your dads as people who are never insecure or afraid of being themselves. Both of you are equally vulnerable and equally needy. Both of you share the same feelings: I want to be loved for who I am—imperfect.

Use these questions to guide your conversation. Write down your answers so that you can reread them whenever you start feeling insecure or pressured to live up to each other's expectations or to be accepted for who you are. Remember to discuss these things in private—just the two of you. And if you can't discuss them in person, then set aside time to have a long phone conversation:

- Tell me two ways in which you don't feel free to be yourself around me.
- What are you afraid would happen if you were more yourself with me?
- What could I do to make you feel more comfortable being yourself with me?
- What do you think each of us is losing by hiding who we are from each other?
- Would you be willing, if I do the same, to tell me just one thing about the real you that you haven't felt free to share?
- What are three expectations that you think I have for you that you're afraid of not living up to?
- What would I have to say or do from here on to convince you that I'm not disappointed in you and I don't expect you to live up to those three expectations?

Dads with Critical or Rejecting Daughters

In some cases a daughter might not only refuse to accept her father for who he is, she might continually criticize or ridicule him for his shortcomings as a parent. She might also ignore or even reject her dad for a period of time—after having criticized him for all his flaws. If that's happening to you as a dad, what can you do? And where do you draw the line in terms of accepting your daughter's harsh judgments and her unwillingness to let go of things you've done wrong in the past? When do you say "enough is enough" when she won't cut you any slack? And how do you stop punishing yourself for your shortcomings as a parent?

First, realize that despite your shortcomings as a father, your daughter is old enough now to be able to weigh the good against the bad. She should be able to accept you as an imperfect, but well-meaning and loving, parent. But if she isn't mature enough to do this, you can't make it happen. What you can do, though, is protect yourself from her verbal assaults. You can let your daughter know that since she has already voiced the same criticisms to you time and time again, there's no point in repeating them. You can also share the guidelines with her from this chapter on how to ask people to change and how to forgive.

Second, don't let your guilt over the mistakes you've made as a parent turn you into a masochist. Just because you screwed up in certain ways doesn't mean you have to give your daughter the power to beat you up emotionally with a constant barrage of criticisms aimed at you. You're not a perfect dad now. And you weren't perfect when you raised her. And if she becomes a parent, she won't be perfect either. Use your guilt as a way to keep you from repeating the mistakes you made in the past as a father, but don't allow your daughter to continually criticize or denigrate you now.

Third, don't assume that just because your daughter is overly critical or may even reject you at times that this means you have done terrible things to her. There are many reasons why adult kids can be overly critical or distant or unkind to their parents. Yes, it might be 50 percent your fault—or even 80 percent your fault. But it might also only be 5 percent or 20 percent your fault. Just don't put all of the blame on yourself.

Finally, it might help if you realize that a number of parents—good parents—feel let down with the way their relationships with their adult children have turned out. Like you, they may feel guilty, disappointed, frustrated, sad, or regretful because what they hoped for isn't what they got:

- I hoped my daughter and I would become good friends, but we haven't.
- Parenting didn't turn out to be the most meaningful experience in my life.
- I thought I could make my daughter happy, but I haven't.
- My daughter doesn't want to be close to me and that hurts.
- She really just doesn't seem to like me very much as a person.
- I thought I'd been a good dad, but she certainly doesn't think so.
- I think someone else might have done a better job raising her than I have.
- My daughter doesn't think much of me as a parent no matter how hard I try.
- No matter how much love I give her, my daughter has never given much in return.

Although your daughter may be overly critical or reject-ing, remember that as she ages—or when she herself becomes a parent—she will probably lighten up on you.

Movies as Catalysts

In terms of improving communication and gaining greater insight into your relationship, I encourage you both to watch the films listed in the next box. You don't necessar-ily have to watch the movies together, though it's a great way to spend an afternoon together at home. If you do watch one of these movies together, try to watch it with-out anyone else around. You'll find that your conversa-tions are more personal and more candid when it's just the two of you. These thought-provoking movies can be cata-lysts to get you talking and thinking about the issues and situations that may be preventing you from communicat-ing in a more meaningful, more honest way with each other.

Consider the ways in which father-daughter relation-ships are affected by the father's relationship with his fa-ther, by the parents' unhappy marriages, and by divorce. And as you're watching each movie, ask yourself: What situations or feelings in this film relate to our family? What ideas or insights could we apply to ourselves as a way of strengthening our relationship? Which scenes were the most meaningful or the most painful in terms of re-minding us of our relationship or our family? Which scenes do we wish would become part of our real-life rela-tionship?

Movies for Fathers and Daughters

Unhappy Marriages and Divorce

Nobody's Fool
Kramer vs. Kramer
Twice in a Lifetime
The Squid and the Whale
Tender Mercies
Ordinary People

Fathers and Sons

I Never Sang for My Father
Pushing Hands
Voyage Around My Father
Tell Me a Riddle
Affliction
King of the Corner

Fathers and Daughters

Father of the Bride
Guess Who's Coming to Dinner
Daddy Nostalgia
Once Around
Eat Drink Man Woman
Pieces of April
Ulee's Gold
The Great Santini
About Schmidt
A Soldier's Daughter Never Cries
One True Thing
On Golden Pond
Slums of Beverly Hills
The Weather Man

Is It Worth It?

Do the ideas in this chapter really work? If you make changes, will you actually notice any improvement in your father-daughter relationship? Yes! Take it from these fathers and daughters:

Anne: *"Now that I tell my father that I do value his opinions, he's stopped giving me so much advice. I almost want him to give me more."*

Tom: *"I don't jump right in there anymore trying to give her ideas for ways to fix her problems. It feels odd. But it makes Anne a lot happier."*

Britta: *"Instead of getting frustrated like I used to when dad would ask me questions, I see now that he's asking because he loves me, not because he's prying."*

Anthony: *"Just the other day I ended up telling her about a few of the ways I screwed up when I was her age. I was afraid she'd see me as weak or stupid. I was shocked when she told me how much she admired me for being who I am. What a relief to know that I don't have to be perfect or a hero in her eyes to be loved."*

Tina: *"I spend a lot more time now talking to him when nobody else is around. He's so much more open and he's really funny!"*

Jack: *"I used to feel that Tina didn't want to spend any time with just me. When I got up the nerve to tell her how much that hurt my feelings, she cried because she was feeling the same way—she thought I didn't want to spend any time alone with her."*

Lucia: *"I've almost stopped crying and walking away every time we disagree about something. He even complimented me on it a few days ago."*

Art: *"I'm a lawyer so I know she was probably right when she said that I intimidated her whenever we argued. I've started saying more positive things to her when we disagree about things. I try not to use my serious lawyer voice!"*

Now let's see how your new ways of communicating can help the two of you get to know each other better.

Getting to Know Each Other 4

❖

- We love each other, but we don't really know each other all that well. I wish we did.
- We don't feel comfortable or relaxed together when it's just the two of us.
- If we had to spend a day together without a television, I have no idea what we'd do.
- I can't imagine our talking about anything personal. It would just feel so weird.
- If only we could forgive each other—or at least apologize.
- I wish we could talk about "it"—that one topic that causes tension for us. But how?
- Why does dad always hand the phone over to mom when I call home?
- I guess it's just not natural for a father and daughter to talk about personal things, right?
- I wish we had a closer relationship, but I don't know how to make that happen.

- *It's not as if we come right out and lie to each other, but we're not exactly honest either about who we are or what we think.*

Knowing You, Not Just Loving You

If you're like most fathers and daughters, you love each other. And that's good news. But you probably don't know each other nearly as well as mom and daughter do. And that's bad news. Why? First, because when you don't know someone well, you are both deprived of a more joyful, more meaningful connection that you might have had throughout your lifetimes together. Second, the one who is left behind when the other dies often feels tremendous guilt or sadness for not having gotten to know the one they loved very well. Third, most of us feel that the greatest compliment anyone can give us is to make a dedicated effort to get to know us better. So at this stage of your lives, let's look at what each of you needs to do to get to know each other better—to move beyond the superficial conversations about sports, television, work, politics, and the weather.

Let's start by having each of you take the "Who Do You Think I Am?" quiz. This quiz is your starting point for getting to know each other better. The better you know one another, the more similar your descriptions will be. Remember: This quiz is not meant to be used as a way to judge or to assess each other's good and bad points. It's meant to help you see how well you know each other, and knowing someone means being able to see both the best and the worst in them. When you finish doing the interviews and activities in this chapter, come back to this checklist to take another look. Odds are, your answers are going to change considerably.

Who Do You Think I Am?

With a pen, rate each adjective that describes you. With a pencil, rate each adjective that describes your father/daughter. Where are your greatest differences and similarities?

0 = never 1 = rarely 2 = usually 3 = almost always/extremely

Positive	Negative
____ hard working	____ underachiever
____ confident/assured	____ low self-esteem
____ self-reliant	____ dependent/needy
____ logical/rational	____ emotional/irrational
____ assertive/outspoken	____ meek/shy
____ forgiving	____ unforgiving
____ nurturing	____ cold/distant
____ considerate	____ inconsiderate/rude
____ reliable/trustworthy	____ unreliable/disloyal
____ unselfish/generous	____ stingy/greedy
____ flexible	____ rigid
____ reflective/introspective	____ shallow
____ frank/straightforward	____ hesitant/passive-aggressive
____ fair/reasonable	____ bossy/domineering
____ accepting/understanding	____ demanding/critical
____ insightful/wise	____ shallow/superficial
____ humble	____ arrogant/boastful
____ open-minded	____ intolerant/judgmental
____ approachable	____ intimidating
____ religious/spiritual	____ non-spiritual
____ relaxed	____ anxious/tense
____ contented	____ dissatisfied/bitter
____ upbeat/optimistic	____ depressed/pessimistic
____ humorous	____ sullen
____ tolerant	____ intolerant

____ **Score**   ____ **Score** (75 possible)

Bad News for Dads and Daughters

- Throughout their lives, most daughters know their mothers better and feel that their mothers know them better than their fathers do.[1-3]
- Most teenagers and young adults talk to their mothers more than their fathers about personal and controversial subjects such as dating, drugs, sex, and drinking.[4, 5]
- When their fathers die, many daughters feel guilty for not having made enough effort to get to know them well.[6, 7]
- Most fathers spend more time with their sons than with their daughters.[8, 9]
- Many children's books, television shows, commercials, and movies send the message that fathers and daughters are not supposed to get to know each other as well as mothers and daughters.[10-13]

Getting to Know Dad: Before It's Too Late

"These days I find myself looking for my father, as though now that he is gone, I might still get to know him better. I miss his personal yet oddly reassuring presence in the world, sitting in his chair in his study with his scholarly books, his round, bald head covered with a flat, black, crocheted yarmulke. 'Write about me,' he said shortly before he died, squeezing my hand, which was his version of a hug."

—Daphne Merkin, essayist and
writer for *The New Yorker*[14]

Only after her father died did Sharona Muir learn by accident that her father had invented Israel's first rocket. Itzhak Bentov sometimes told his daughter stories about his life as a young man, but she never

[84]

knew he had been a member of a top-secret group of scientists making weapons for Israel's War of Independence. Amazed by what she discovered, Muir went to Israel after her father's death to meet the people he had known and to get to know her father by writing about his life in her first book, *The Book of Telling*.[15]

Equal Opportunity Fathers and Daughters

As father and daughter, you both need to dump the negative, sexist stereotypes—those myths and half truths that have kept you from giving each other the opportunities to share more meaningful, personal things—that we've discussed in earlier chapters. Remember: Men and women are more alike than they are different when it comes to how they communicate, what they feel, and what they want to talk about in a meaningful relationship. Remember, too, that fathers and daughters can and should have just as personal and just as meaningful a relationship as fathers and sons. Use the "Are You an Equal Opportunity Father or Daughter" quiz to see how you can create more opportunities to get to know each other.

Spending Time Together

When is the last time the two of you spent time together without anyone else around? When did you last talk on the phone for more than five minutes without someone else on the line? Come to think about it, since your daughter became a teenager, how often have the two of you done anything together without mom or the other siblings there too? Now think back to the one-on-one time you spent together before those teenage years, those special times for just the two of you, memories that only the two of you share. What happened? Why did your special father-daughter times end?

QUIZ

Are You an Equal Opportunity
Father or Daughter?

Compared to the way you treat your mother, how much opportunity have you taken to get to know your father? Compared to the way you treat your son, how much opportunity have you taken to get to know your daughter?

0 = never   1 = rarely   2 = usually   3 = almost always

Daughter Dad

_____ _____ I share as much about what's going on in my life as I do with mom/my son.

_____ _____ I invite him/her to do things alone with me.

_____ _____ I ask personal or meaningful questions.

_____ _____ I make sure my father/daughter knows how much I value his/her opinion.

_____ _____ I ask what's going on in the other person's life besides work.

_____ _____ We shop or do errands together.

_____ _____ We talk about feelings, not just about opinions and ideas.

_____ _____ We ask for advice on personal matters.

_____ _____ We write, phone, or send emails just to each other.

_____ _____ We talk about our past together and about our own experiences in the past.

_____ _____ We let each other know what we'd like more of in our relationship.

_____ _____ I act interested and enthusiastic when asked about my life.

_____ _____ I buy gifts that show how well I know him/her.

_____ _____ I get in touch just to ask how he/she is doing.

_____ _____ I say "I love you."

_____ _____ **Your scores** (45 possible)

As we discussed in a previous chapter, the sad reality is that most fathers and daughters follow society's script. And the script says once a daughter becomes a teenager, a father is supposed to back off and stop spending time alone with his daughter the way they used to do when she was a child. But it's never too late to dump the script and write a new one of your own. The first step in getting to know each other better is to spend more time together without other people around— the way you used to do. But as simple as this sounds, if you aren't used to being alone with each other, it's going to feel uncomfortable at first. So ease into it by doing these sorts of activities together:

- Go to a religious service.
- Run errands and stop for coffee.
- Walk through a park and watch kids at the playground.
- Go to a movie.
- Teach each other how to do something: trim plants, grill steaks, play cards.
- Go back to the neighborhood where dad grew up and walk around together.
- Visit the cemetery where a relative or friend is buried.
- Go off for a few hours to take pictures of places that mean a lot to both of you.

Why is it so important to have this one-on-one time? Well, let's think about that. Other than with each other, think back to your last meaningful or personal conversation with someone. Who else was participating in that talk? Odds are it was just the two of you. Right? Where were you? Odds are you were someplace private and quiet where other people couldn't overhear what you were saying and where nobody could interrupt or distract you. Right? How much time had you spent together that day before you got into that memorable conversation? Probably several hours, yes? In other words, if you want to get to know each other at a deeper level, you need privacy and time—no audience and no rushing. Why not turn your fantasy of "The Perfect Day Together" into reality?

The Perfect Day Together

- What would be a perfect day together?
- Where would the two of you go?
- What would you do?
- Where would you have lunch?
- What would you do to make each other feel special?
- How would each of you feel at the end of the day?
- What would you each say that you've never said before?
- What inexpensive gift would you give as a token of your love?
- What are the last words each of you would say to the other at the end of the day?

What about mom? How will she react to the two of you spending time together without her? For reasons we'll discuss in the next chapter, many moms feel jealous, hurt, or left out when father and daughter begin spending more time together. Fathers and daughters are often aware of this, as Janet explains:

> "Before I started to ask my father the questions in this chapter, he said half jokingly, 'I'll tell you one thing: the

only way I'll answer the questions is if you-know-who isn't around.' Of course, he was talking about my mother, and he said it while all three of us were standing in the kitchen. We all laughed, even my mom. But his simple comment drove home to me the importance of establishing equal but separate relationships with my parents. He wanted to tell his stories to his daughter without my mom piping in with, 'Wait, wait you've got that all wrong ... oh, you forgot to tell her. . . .' From now on I'm making a promise to myself not to treat him like a second-rate parent. When I have something to tell him, I'll find time alone with him or I'll call him at work so we can have our privacy."

If you sense that mom is jealous or feels hurt when you don't always include her in your father-daughter conversations, or when you two go out together without her, you've got several options. First, as a daughter or as a father, you can sweetly and patiently explain to mom that because mother and daughter have gotten to know each other so well, it's important for father and daughter to "catch up before it's too late." It's unlikely that mom will resent or disapprove of a request that's presented like that. Second, you can create private father-daughter time without always taking time away from mom. For example, you can plan phone calls when mom isn't going to be home or when dad is at work, send emails through dad's business address, and run errands or share recreational activities that mom has no interest in. A round of golf can turn into a whole day with a long, leisurely lunch and very little golf. A quick errand can be extended by a long coffee break or long walk. Third, take every opportunity that comes along for driving somewhere together—picking each other up at the airport, running errands, going to visit a relative. Some of your most meaningful talks will happen in those *uninter-rupted* hours driving somewhere together.

Mom: Always Interrupting?

"I was listening to my father attentively when, out of the blue, Mother, her voice strident, began to talk too—interrupting him, overriding him, pointing out some peculiarity in the shoes he had on. We all fell silent. It was so strikingly odd and rude, what she'd done. So desperate. I remember this because the whole event seemed an apt metaphor for what had happened in my relationship with my father—in my ability to talk to him, to know him. It had been interrupted. For years it had been interrupted by Mother's desperation, by her need to be the absolute center of attention."

—Sue Miller, award-winning novelist, from her
memoir *The Story of My Father*[16]

Meaningful Questions

Spending time together probably isn't going to help you get to know each other a lot better unless you use that time to ask more personal, more meaningful questions. Think of it this way: Your chances of catching the kind of fish you want is greater when you use the right kind of bait. I can bait you with these questions: "What's new?" or "How you doing?" Or I can bait you with these questions: "What's been the best and worst part of your week?" or "How did you feel about the family re-union?" If I'm fishing for ways to get to know you better, the second bait is far better than the first. The questions in the following section are good bait—use them!

Another way to jump-start personal conversations is to

choose ten to fifteen photographs that you especially like from various times of your lives. Dad, be sure to include pictures of yourself as a child, teenager, and young man. Daughter, be sure to include some pictures that include people your father doesn't know. Find a quiet, *private* place where *just the two of you* can spend at least an hour looking at the pictures together. Tell each other what was going in each picture and explain why you chose that particular picture. Why was it meaningful or special to you? You can help each other along by asking questions such as: What was that like? Why did it turn out that way? How did that make you feel? What happened next? How did that happen? What was going on before then? How do you feel about that now?

If the two of you can't get together to answer the questions in person, you can talk about them on the phone or in emails. It might make you more comfortable if you email the questions to each other so you'll have time to think about your answers. Dads, if you're not used to talking to your daughter about personal things, you might be tempted to brush her off with: "Oh, just get your mom to tell you about that," or "I don't remember." Give this a chance. Remember, your daughter probably had to get her nerve up to ask you these questions. This is your chance to give her the gift of getting to know you—and to give yourself the gift of getting to know her.

Who Are You? Who Am I?

Childhood and Family
1. Who is (or was) your favorite relative? Why?
2. What do you like most about your parents and grandparents?
3. How are you like and unlike your parents?

4. What are two of your favorite childhood memories?
5. When you were a child, how did each of your parents show they loved you?
6. As a child and teenager, what were some of your most peaceful moments? Most jealous? Angriest? Most tragic? Most desperate? Happiest? Proudest? Most embarrassing? Most frightening?
7. What did you get too little of as a child? What did you get too much of?
8. How did your relationship with your parents change during your teenage years?
9. What have you had to forgive your father for? And your mother?
10. How are you and your siblings alike and different? Why do you think that is?
11. What is something you wish, or would have wished, for your father? Your mother?
12. What were some of your favorite childhood toys or games?
13. Who were your best friends as a child and teenager?
14. Other than a relative, who was especially kind to you as a child and a teenager?
15. What was your best and your worst birthday as a child?

Values
1. What book, film, and piece of music have affected you a lot, and why?
2. What's your favorite time of day, and why?
3. If you had a motto, what would it be?
4. If you could afford it, what would you buy or do?
5. What do you wish you had more of, and why?
6. What are your three most important possessions?
7. How do you define yourself politically?
8. Other than family members, which three people do you admire, and why?

9. If you could change any two laws, what would they be?
10. What would bring you the greatest joy during the next few years?

Friends

1. What are four traits you look for in a friend?
2. Who have you known longest and why has your friendship lasted so long?
3. Which friend do you miss most, and why?
4. What is the best advice a friend ever gave you?
5. Which friend knows you the best and which one is the most different from you?
6. What have friends done that hurt you the most and how did you deal with that?
7. What does it take for you to forgive a friend?
8. What things do you have the hardest time forgiving?
9. How do you show love and anger to your friends?
10. What do your friends like most and least about you?
11. What have you learned about friendship over the years?
12. What do you feel bad about doing to a friend?
13. What are some of the best things your friends have done for you?
14. How have your friendships changed as you have aged?
15. What are some of your saddest experiences with friends?

Spiritual Beliefs

1. How have your religious beliefs changed over time?
2. What are some of your most spiritual experiences?
3. What spiritual questions do you ask yourself most often?
4. How would you like to spend the last year of your life?
5. Other than relatives, who would you like to see during the last years of your life?
6. What do you hope people will remember most about you?

7. How would you want your funeral arranged?
8. What are your greatest worries about aging or dying?
9. How has someone's death affected your spiritual views?
10. What role does organized religion play in your life?

How You See Yourself

1. How successful do you think you are? Why?
2. What are some of your best and worst traits?
3. How do you think you developed those traits?
4. What are some of the best compliments you've ever gotten?
5. What do you wish you had done differently in regard to your work?
6. What are some of the best and the worst decisions you've ever made?
7. What are two of the most unselfish things you've ever done?
8. What lessons have you learned the hard way?
9. What do you wish you could change about yourself? Why?

Love and Romance

1. What are some of your best and worst dating experiences?
2. How do you feel about people living together or having sex before marriage?
3. How do you feel about gay and lesbian relationships?
4. What romantic relationship had the greatest impact on you and how?
5. What do you wish had been different about your romantic relationships?
6. How liberal or conservative do you consider yourself to be on sexual issues?
7. How have your ideas about love, sex, and marriage changed over time?
8. What do you wish you had known about love when you were younger?

9. What are your strengths and weaknesses in a relationship?
10. What were some heartbreaking experiences you had in your romantic life?

Biracial Daughters

Getting to know each other can be especially complicated for those daughters who have one white parent and one African American parent. These interracial marriages tend to be more frowned upon than marriages between other races, which can put a greater strain on the father-daughter relationship. If your family is biracial, you already know how this can enrich your relationship—or how it can strain and sometimes destroy it. As you can see from the stories in Biracial Daughters and Their Dads, many biracial daughters never know their fathers because their parents separated and didn't stay in touch. Others only get to know their dads late in life. But others do have an ongoing, loving connection. These daughters' books can help you gain more insight into your relationship—where it has been and where it might go from here. And their books can help you get to know each other better, even if you have had very little contact until now.

Biracial Daughters and Their Dads

Mariah Carey, award-winning singer

Carey's mother is a white Irish American who was an opera singer and raised Mariah on her own. Her father, an African American/Venezuelan, had very little contact with Carey after her parents divorced when she was three, but father and daughter stayed in touch.

In his later life, he and Mariah reconciled. After his death, she wrote *Sunflowers for Alfred Roy* in his honor:[17]

> Please be at peace father
> I'm at peace with you
> Bitterness isn't worth clinging to
> After all the anguish we've been through

Essie Washington, author

In *Dear Senator: Memoir of the Daughter of Strom Thurmond*, Essie Mae Washington-Williams, at the age of seventy-eight, finally told the truth about her parents. After her one-hundred-year-old father died, Washington wrote a book about her black mother, Carrie Butler, and white father, South Carolina Senator Strom Thurmond. The senator was a national leader who vehemently opposed integration. Essie found out when she sixteen that the "aunt" who was raising her was actually her mother—and that her father was the rich white lawyer Strom Thurmond, who would later become a senator, governor, and presidential candidate. Washington's mother was a fifteen-year-old black maid who was working for the Thurmond family when twenty-three-year-old Strom had an affair with her. (Carrie died at thirty-eight in a hospital poverty ward.) Essie first met her dad when she was seventeen. According to her, he was financially generous and affectionate. But he never acknowledged her publicly as his daughter. All of their meetings and letters were kept secret. Washington writes, "Every girl wants her daddy and I wanted mine . . . I believed he loved me, after his fashion. . . . I am every bit as white as I am black, and it is my full intention to drink the nectar of both goblets."[18]

June Cross, Emmy award–winning producer and author

In *Secret Daughter: A Mixed Race Daughter and the Mother Who Gave Her Away*, June Cross writes about her life as the daughter of a white woman and a well-known black vaudeville star, Jimmy Cross. After Cross's parents split up when she was four, her mom married an emerging Hollywood star. She sent June away to be raised by a black family, fearing that her husband's career would be destroyed since June's skin was too dark for her to "pass" as white. While producing a documentary about her life after her dad's death, June went to Harlem and discovered home movies of him standing outside the Apollo Theater holding a baby: "It took me a couple of replays before it hit me . . . *that baby was me*. This is the only picture of us I've ever seen. I played it again and again."[19]

Lise Funderburg, author

In her book *Pig Candy: Taking My Father South, Taking My Father Home*, the daughter of a white mother and black father writes about her family. Funderburg could never understand why her dad was so strict and so elusive while she was growing up. But when she was forty, she learned he was dying of cancer. She took him on several trips back to his hometown in Jasper County, Georgia. In discovering her father's past, she discovered the warmth, humor, and wonder of her father, especially when, in his final months, he brought family and friends together to throw a pig roast.[20]

How to Discuss "It"

Getting to know each other also means, at some point, trying to talk about "It"—that one topic that is still creating tension or anger in your relationship, no matter how long ago it happened. Your "It" might be alcoholism, depression, adultery, cancer, anorexia, divorce, death, dad's tour in Vietnam or Iraq, sex, religion. Whatever "It" is, one or both of you doesn't know how to bring it up. You're afraid. Afraid of what? Until you figure that out, you can't get "It" out into the open. So which of these things are you afraid might happen if you try to talk about "It"?

- Our relationship might get worse.
- One or both of us might cry.
- We might be embarrassed.
- We might not know what to say next.
- Dad might cut me off financially.
- We might not respect each other as much.
- We might yell or get angry.
- Other people in the family will get upset with us.
- I might fall off the pedestal the person has me on.

Now use the "Why Am I Afraid" quiz on page 100 to figure out exactly what you're afraid of. Then try to imagine the best and worst outcomes—and the likelihood of any happening. Maybe these two daughters' experiences will help you put aside your fears and have that conversation.

Lindsey: *"I was extremely nervous to talk to my dad about his having had prostate cancer last year. I presumed he would feel uncomfortable talking about some-*

thing so personal. Surprisingly he didn't skip a beat. Letting him know how frightened I had been was such a relief, but hearing his side of the story was much more significant. His openness in talking about such a difficult topic gives me confidence to go to him with serious, complicated problems from now on. His ability to put me at ease was so incredible and so surprising."

Meredith: *"I always knew that my parents had a baby who had died before I was born. I never thought I should ask about it. But finally I did. I had never heard my dad talk like he did that night with me. I could see the hurt in his eyes and hear the shakiness in his voice, even after so many years. Suddenly I understood why my dad had always been such a germ freak. It stemmed from the baby's death, because nobody ever figured out why she had died. Dad said the one question he would like to ask God is why He took away his baby. As dad and I were talking, I realized that I have believed those negative stereotypes about fathers that you talked to me about. I was so wrong to assume he wouldn't want to talk about his weaknesses or the times in life when he was hurt."*

Discussing Your Relationship

Sometimes "It" is your desire to talk about ways to improve your father-daughter relationship. What do each of you wish was different? How could you make those things happen? What do you each want more of, and what do you want less of? As a daughter, use the questions in the "Our Father-Daughter Relationship" section to talk with your dad about your relationship.

Why Am I Afraid to Talk About "It"?

These are three things I'd like us to discuss if I knew the outcome would be good:

1. _____
2. _____
3. _____

The worst things I can imagine happening if we talked are:

1. _____
2. _____
3. _____

How likely is it that each of those bad things would happen?
1 = very unlikely   2 = 50/50 chance   3 = definitely

1. _____
2. _____
3. _____

The most positive things I can imagine happening if we talked are:

1. _____
2. _____
3. _____

How likely is it that each of the three best things might happen?
1 = very unlikely   2 = 50/50 chance   3 = definitely

1. _____
2. _____
3. _____

Our Father-Daughter Relationship

Fatherhood

1. What has been the most fun about being a father?
2. How has being a father changed you?
3. As a young father, what worried you the most?
4. What do you wish you had known before you became a father?
5. How well do you think you fit our society's definition of a "good" father?
6. What are your greatest strengths and weaknesses as a father?
7. How did your relationship with your dad influence the kind of parent you have been?
8. What advice would you give to younger fathers?
9. How has being a father to a son been different from being a father to a daughter?
10. How have your ideas and your behavior as a father changed over the years?

Our Relationship

1. What was the best gift and best compliment I ever gave you?
2. What was hard about being my father when I was an infant? A teenager? Now?
3. How has our relationship changed since my childhood?
4. What do you wish we had more of in our relationship now?
5. What do you wish we had done differently in our relationship?
6. What do you enjoy most about our relationship now?
7. What do you wish I understood better about you?

[101]

8. What are some of the saddest and happiest experiences you've had with me?
9. What questions do you wish I had asked you about our relationship?
10. What questions are you glad I didn't ask you? (You don't have to answer them.)

Wish Lists

What three things do we enjoy most about our relationship?

Daughter	**Dad**
1. _____	
2. _____	
3. _____	

What three things would each of us like changed or improved?

Daughter	**Dad**
1. _____	
2. _____	
3. _____	

What three things could each of us do differently to strengthen our relationship?

Daughter	**Dad**
1. _____	
2. _____	
3. _____	

Lies and Deception

Many fathers and daughters have a hard time getting to know each other better because of the lies and deception that have become part of their relationship. "Ah, what a tangled web we weave, when first we practice to deceive." Some of us try to excuse our lies and deception by telling ourselves: "I'm not lying, I'm just protecting my privacy. Besides, fathers and daughters shouldn't tell each other everything about their lives." True, privacy is a good thing. For example, we don't want other people reading our mail, eavesdropping on our conversations, rummaging through our things, or walking into our bedroom or bathroom without knocking. And true, no two people in any relationship should tell each other everything about their lives. *But privacy doesn't mean deceiving or lying to each other and privacy doesn't mean pretending to be someone other than who you are.*

Let's consider Fred and Rose, who both claim they're not lying to each other. Fred has told countless lies over the years because he doesn't want his thirty-year-old daughter Rose to know that he had a child before he met her mother. And he has sworn his wife to secrecy to hide this information from Rose. That's not privacy—that's deception. And Rose is deceiving Fred, her very religious father, because she doesn't want him to discover that she has been an atheist for years. She pretends that religion is a vital part of her life by going to church with her father when she visits and by talking as though she is actively involved in her church at home. That's not a little white lie—that's deception.

Unlike Fred and Rose, you can be honest about who you are and what you believe without disclosing the intimate details of your private life. You can maintain your privacy without being an imposter by saying things like: *"Yes, I had a child before*

I met your mother, but I don't feel comfortable telling you any more about that part of my life." "Dad, I no longer believe in God so I don't practice a religion anymore. Because I consider this a very private matter, I don't want to talk about it in any more detail."

Deceiving each other hurts your father-daughter relationship because at some point you're asking yourself: Would this person love me as much if he or she knew the "real" me? What will happen if the "real" me is discovered? How much longer can I go on being a phony? Let's face it; most of us know the difference between privacy and deception. When you deceive someone, you feel guilty—that tight feeling in your chest, the tense neck, the queasy stomach. When you go to great lengths to hide information or to pretend to believe things you don't believe in, then you're being deceptive and dishonest—not private. Privacy doesn't detract from your father-daughter relationship. Deception and dishonesty do.

How about secrecy? Is that deception? Is there any harm in sharing personal information with someone else in the family but not with each other? Let's think about that. As a father, how would you feel if your daughter told her mother something extremely important but neither woman let you in on their "little" secret? And as a daughter, how would you feel if your father shared something extremely important with your sister but not with you? It's just their "little" secret. No harm done, right? Wrong. When you share important or personal information with someone you love but exclude someone else you love, the message is clear: I don't trust you as much or feel as close to you as I do to the other person.

Even when the hidden information isn't very earthshattering, the person being excluded feels like an outsider. And it hurts to be treated like an outsider. Forget about your father-daughter relationship for a minute. How do you feel when your close friend shares a secret with someone else, but not with you? How do you feel when you're the last one to be let in on the secret? What if your friend has told the secret to almost everyone else except you? Even if the secret information was trivial, how does being left out make you feel about your friendship?

The other problem with secrets is that fathers and daughters sometimes start out keeping secrets about little things. But as the years pass, those little secrets become bigger secrets. The young girl and mom who keep secrets from dad about how much money they spend on their shopping sprees might end up being the adult daughter and mother who keep much bigger secrets from dad: the daughter being raped, having an eating disorder, being clinically depressed, having a drinking problem, having an abortion. And yes, there are daughters and mothers who keep such secrets from dear old dad while telling themselves, "We're not lying to him. It's just that he would get upset. He wouldn't be able to handle it."

As you take the "Privacy or Deception?" quiz on the next page, ask yourself if anyone in your family is encouraging you to keep secrets from each other. These people may mean well, but their advice isn't likely to strengthen your father-daughter relationship.

Apologizing and Forgiving

As you're getting to know each other better, you might discover that you have some apologizing and forgiving to do. What does it mean to forgive? For me, forgiving doesn't mean forgetting or pretending certain things never happened. Forgiving means being willing to stop punishing the other person—to stop withholding love, refusing to talk to them, asking them to apologize again and again, or reminding them

Privacy or Deception?

How truthful are you with each other about these aspects of your lives?

0 = not at all   1 = sometimes

2 = half the time   3 = almost always

Dad Daughter

_____ _____ financial matters

_____ _____ drinking

_____ _____ mental health problems

_____ _____ smoking

_____ _____ political beliefs

_____ _____ health problems

_____ _____ job or school problems

_____ _____ religious beliefs

_____ _____ your romantic life

When you aren't being honest with each other, what do you usually do to hide the truth?

Dad Daughter

_____ _____ change the topic

_____ _____ withhold information

_____ _____ tell a half truth

_____ _____ conceal the evidence so as not to get caught

_____ _____ mislead, distort, or misrepresent

_____ _____ lie

repeatedly about their mistake. Forgiving means confronting some tough questions: Why aren't you willing to let the other person off the hook? How long do you plan to stay angry and to keep punishing them? A year? Ten years? A lifetime? Is staying angry a way to blame the other person for everything that goes wrong in your life instead of assuming responsibility yourself? Just exactly what would the person have to do in order to win your forgiveness? Have you told them? If not, why not?

Forgiveness isn't a gift you give the other person. *It's a gift you give yourself.* Until you forgive, you can't move forward in the relationship. You deprive yourself of the greater joy the person can offer you. You also deprive yourself of the peaceful feeling that comes from letting go of the anger. As the saying goes, "Anger is never without a reason—but seldom a good one."

Have you ever felt that you did apologize but weren't forgiven? How can that be? Part of the problem is that what feels like an apology to you might not feel like a sincere apology to the other person. Thinking back to your apology, ask yourself how well you did each of these six things:

1) Don't shift the blame. Don't say, "I'm sorry, but if you hadn't done such and such then I wouldn't have done such and such." Instead, accept full responsibility for what *you did.* "I'm sorry. It was my fault. I don't have any excuse for what I did."

2) Don't apologize for hurting the person's feelings. Don't say, "I'm sorry that your feelings are hurt." Instead, apologize for what *you did.* "I'm sorry that I drank too much and embarrassed you."

3) Don't trivialize the damage you did. Don't say, "It was really no big deal. I don't know why you're so upset." Instead, accept how the other person feels. "I realize how much I hurt you. And I am truly sorry."

4) Don't take the focus away from the other person's feelings by talking about how awful you feel about what you did. Don't say, "I feel so guilty. I haven't been able to sleep for a week. I don't know how I'm ever going to get over this." Instead, focus on the other person's feelings. "I can see how heartbroken you are. I realize how much stress I have caused you."

5) Don't criticize while you're apologizing. Don't say, "I'm sorry I behaved that way, but you've done the same thing to me. Why just last week..."

6) Don't just apologize. Try to *do something* to repair the damage or to make the other person feel better. If you don't know what to do, ask!

If you feel the other person owes you an apology, here's my question: Are you *absolutely* certain that the other person *knows* that you feel you're due an apology? And are you 100 percent sure that he or she knows *exactly* what the wrongdoing was? As odd as these questions sound, many fathers and daughters have not let one another know that they are hurt or angry and that they want an apology. One person is angry or hurt and the other is totally unaware that there's a problem. As Meg says, "If dad can't figure out what he did wrong and that he owes me an apology, then I'm not going to tell him." And as Joe says, "My daughter is old enough to know that she hurt me and that she needs to say she's sorry. It's her responsibility to bring this up, not mine." Both Meg and Joe are taking the "you know what you did and you're refusing to apologize" approach.

But this isn't necessarily a smart assumption. Why not? Because sometimes we're truly not aware of what we've done that has upset the other person. We're in the dark. And the person who hasn't forgiven us refuses to shed any light on what's going on. That's just not fair. So if you feel someone owes you an apology, for pity's sake tell the poor soul so that he or she has a chance to get out of the doghouse. Second, sometimes we don't apologize because we're afraid that, once we admit we did wrong, the other person will "hold it against me" or "use it against me." Not only is this highly unlikely, but by *not* apologizing, you've got a 100 percent guarantee that the other person *will* hold it against you.

As a daughter or as a father, you might not realize the ways in which you have hurt each other's feelings or made each other feel unloved or unimportant—things you have said or done in the past and might still be doing now. So it's time that one of you takes the lead now—assume the initiative to talk about these questions. Just remember, you two need to be alone when you have this conversation. Give yourselves plenty of time. Reassure each other that you really do want honesty—and that neither of you is going to get mad or defensive. So here goes:

- Tell me about times that I have hurt your feelings or made you feel unimportant, overlooked, left out, or unappreciated. What do you wish I had done instead?
- What gift have I given you that made you feel I didn't really know you well? What could I have given you instead?
- On holidays or on your birthday, what could I have done differently to make you feel more loved, more appreciated, or more important?
- Have you ever seen another father or daughter do something for each other that you wish we were doing for each other?

Apologizing and Forgiving

What three things could each of you apologize for that might strengthen your relationship?

Daughter   **Father**

1._____   1._____

2._____   2._____

3._____   3._____

What are three reasons why each of you hasn't apologized?

1._____   1._____

2._____   2._____

3._____   3._____

In addition to an apology, what could each of you do to be forgiven?

1._____   1._____

2._____   2._____

3._____   3._____

When I think about forgiveness, I think about Jill, whose dad had almost torn their family apart because of his heavy drinking when Jill was young. As a thirty-year-old woman, Jill was asking her dad about his life. "When I asked my father what the best gift I ever gave him was, he told me it was a paper on forgiveness that I had written in high school. I had almost forgotten about it. But to him it was the most special thing I have ever done for him because in the paper I let him know that I had forgiven him for the problems he caused our family. I believe that everyone has the right to be forgiven if they are truly remorseful—and my father was. Good people make bad decisions sometimes. My relationship with my father has just grown stronger over the years because we love each other despite mistakes we have both made."

Is It Worth It?

If you follow through on the suggestions in this chapter, will it be worth it? Here is what daughters say after they have spent time alone with their fathers discussing the "getting to know you" questions in this chapter.

Sue: *"I had never seen pictures of my father as a child—so small and vulnerable. When I got him talking about his dad, I saw him fight not to show me his pain. I actually reached over to him and said it was okay to talk to me about it. It was such a weird moment—me reaching out to my dad for the first time."*

Jody: *"As I got him to talk about his childhood, I realized that my dad was a victim of vicious cycles in his own family. It's hard now to be angry with him over things he never learned how to do. The thing that glaringly stood out for me was how negative an impact my grandfather had on dad. My dad still seems to be trying to prove to his dead father that he can be successful."*

Joanne: *"His stories were so meaningful because I am struggling with the same questions as he did when he was my age. I also saw him as a young man remembering what it was like to fall in love. There was such tenderness in his voice."*

Jen: *"As I listened to him, I was finally able to imagine him as a twenty-one-year-old with no responsibility or medical initials after his name—young and jovial, playing the drums, eyeing the girls. He used to dream of being a free spirit, a famous athlete, and a wealthy tycoon. Who knew?"*

Lynne: *"The more questions I asked, the more I saw my father as a person who struggles through life as a man and a husband—not just as my father. When we were discussing his dreams, the expressive look on his face and his tone of voice made me see him as a man with a lonely heart. It meant so much to have him open up to me."*

Paula: *"I was surprised to learn that he still sees his life as a developing process, even at his age. I'd never thought he was introspective and now I find out he is. We actually talked about religion for more than an hour. I don't know why I haven't asked him these questions before."*

Sally: *"When I first told my dad I wanted to spend a few hours alone with him to ask questions about his life, he laughed and seemed very nervous. But he did it. It ended up being the first time we've ever talked about his life for more than ten minutes."*

Marty: *"As we talked, I realized that he and I have been wanting the same thing from our relationship all these years. But we never talked enough to figure that out."*

Anna: *"It was very moving when my dad said the nicest gift I ever gave him was deciding finally that I want to get to know him."*

Work and Money: Minefields and Misunderstandings

5

❖

- *We're always arguing about money. Why can't he loosen up?*
- *My daughter treats me like a bank machine. When will she grow up?*
- *Dad seemed to care more about his job than about me when I was growing up.*
- *Why can't my daughter appreciate what I have done for her financially?*
- *I hate the way he gripes at mom when he gets home from work.*
- *When I was her age, I already had a good job. Why can't she settle into something?*
- *He acts as if paying for my wedding is bankrupting him. Why is he ruining this for me?*
- *Sometimes my daughter seems to care more about my money than about me.*

Men's Money, Women's Love

Do these comments ring a bell? Probably so, because money and work have a big impact on most dads' relationships with their daughters. Let's start with this sad reality: Many men believe that the amount of money they earn affects the way women feel about them. Dad, now's your chance to share your experiences and your feelings about money and fear—a man's fear of losing a woman's love if he loses his job or never earns as much as she expected him to, his fear of not finding a woman who will love him because he's not as rich as the next guy, his fear of not being admired as much as the other dads because he can't buy his daughter the things that they can. As a daughter, this might sound like nonsense. But then, you're not a man. Yes, it's possible that your dad doesn't feel this way. But the fact remains: Millions of fathers do believe that earning plenty of money is the yardstick used to measure them as husbands and fathers. And if he fails to measure up, he fears losing his family's admiration or respect.[1-3]

So, are fathers right? Do some daughters and wives love or admire men partly for their money? Seems so. For instance, in a recent survey most college students said that making money was a major part of being a good father.[4] And daughters whose dads help them financially as adults are more likely to take care of their fathers in old age than daughters who don't get any money from their dads.[5] Yes, women usually marry men whose incomes are higher than theirs. Rarely does a woman "marry down" by marrying a man from a lower economic class than hers.[6] Not surprisingly, only 20 percent of wives earn more than their husbands.[7] And the closer a man's wife's income gets to his, the worse a man often feels about himself as a husband.[8] There's also a connection between a man's money and his wife having the freedom not to work. Only half of the wives whose husbands earn more than $120,000 a year work, usually part-time, compared to 80 percent of other wives.[9] And too many of us criticize and judge men far more harshly than women if they don't earn "enough" for their families.[10]

We might want to deny these uncomfortable realities. But it's hard to deny the messages that bombard us in most movies and television shows: a man's money does matter—a lot. Think about these blockbuster movies and television series: *My Big Fat Greek Wedding*, *Desperate Housewives*, *Maid in Manhattan*, *Father of the Bride*, and *The Sopranos*. Now ask yourself: Did these wives and daughters seem to be enjoying dad's money—the fancy restaurants, vacations, big houses, expensive cars, lavish weddings? For sure! For decades most movies have shown that dad's role is to buy things for his daughter—and the more he buys, the more she loves and admires him.[11]

Now what does this have to do with your father-daughter relationship? Just this: If you believe that the "best" dads have to earn plenty of money, then dad is going to spend a lot of time away from his family trying to live up to that expectation. More money equals less time with his daughter. Pretty simple. Sadly, too many daughters grow up expecting dad to show his love with money—an expensive wedding, her own car, a private college education, a horse, a down payment on her house. If dad can't measure up, then what? And if he does measure up, what exactly is it that we've measured—his paycheck or his love?

Damaging Myths: Demeaning Our Dads

Not only do a number of men feel that their wives and daughters admire or respect them more for earning lots of money, but many damaging myths are floating around about

QUIZ

Fooling Yourself? Men, Work, and Family

What do you believe (true or false)?

Dad Daughter

_____ _____ Most men enjoy their work as much or more than they enjoy their kids.

_____ _____ When both parents work full-time, dads still spend much less time with kids than mom.

_____ _____ In the United States, men have historically earned all the money while women raised the kids.

_____ _____ Most dads wouldn't take weeks off work to stay home with their newborns even if the law allowed it.

_____ _____ Dads usually have more free time for themselves than moms do.

_____ _____ Most men enjoy their jobs more than women do.

_____ _____ Most kids wish their mom could stay home instead of having to work.

_____ _____ The main reason dads don't spend more time with their kids is because men aren't as interested in kids as women are.

_____ _____ Employed mothers are more stressed than fathers trying to balance work and family.

_____ _____ Dads usually have closer relationships with the kids when mom is a homemaker.

_____ _____ **Total True** (10 possible)

[116]

how dads feel about their jobs and their families. Let's see how many of these myths you two believe in the "Fooling Yourself?" quiz.

How many did you think were true? Hopefully, zero. All are false, as you can see from the research in "The Dad Report Card: Passing or Failing?" and "Employed Moms" sections that follow. The problem is that daughters can fall for many of the negative myths about dads that are so popular in our country such as the myth that dads do far less childcare and work at home than moms. Or the myth that most dads choose to work as much as they do because they enjoy their jobs as much as—or more than—they enjoy their kids. Imagine how mothers would feel if such nonsense was being spread about them instead of about fathers. That's why it's important to become familiar with the facts. You can refuse to be part of the rumor mill that spreads such mean gossip about dads. Next time someone starts spouting the kind of baloney that's in the "Fooling Yourself?" quiz, speak up! Set them straight with the research and statistics.

The Dad Report Card: Passing or Failing?

Dads at Work

- 80 percent of dads earn most of the money for the family—of those, 20 percent earn all of it.[12]
- Counting housework, childcare, and paid work, most mothers only work forty-one hours a week while most fathers work fifty-one hours.[13]
- On average, men spend ten more hours a week at work than employed women.[14]
- Dads struggle as much as employed moms to balance the demands of work and family.[15, 16]

- Historically in the "traditional" family in the United States, both parents have worked to support the family.[17]

Dads at Home

- Dads are spending more time than ever with their kids, roughly 20 percent less than moms.[18]
- Today's moms and dads work longer hours and do less housework than their parents did.[19]
- Younger fathers are more likely than older fathers to say they would give up part of their income to spend more time at home with the kids.[20]
- Today's mothers spend less time doing housework and more time working outside the home, and fathers spend more time than ever before on housework and with the kids.[21]
- When Sweden passed laws in 1999 to encourage dads to take childcare leaves of absence, the leaves increased from 3 percent to 36 percent.[22]

Employed Moms

- The more hours a mom works outside the home, the more time dad usually spends with the kids.[23]
- Nearly 40 percent of moms with preschool kids work full-time; 20 percent work part-time.[24]
- More than 50 percent of moms with school-aged kids work full-time; 25 percent work part-time.[25]
- Employed mothers have lower divorce rates than wives whose husbands earn all of the family's money.[26]
- When moms work night shifts, dads and kids have a closer relationship without affecting how close the kids are to their mom.[27]
- Most young adults whose mothers were housewives

wished she had been employed, and 80 percent of those whose mothers had jobs were glad she did.[28]

Dad's Job: Impact on Daughters

In addition to the damaging myths about dads and work, your relationship is also influenced by the decisions that dad and mom made when they first married. Who would earn most of the family's money? Who would spend the most time with the kids? Meredith's and Jeanette's parents exemplify the two extremes.

Long before her parents ever met, Meredith's future mother had decided that she didn't want a career that would be too demanding. She mainly wanted to be a stay-at-home mom. After she married, she worked while her young husband finished law school and fulfilled his father's dream of becoming a lawyer. When Meredith was born, her mom quit work while her dad climbed his way up the ladder to become a partner in a top-notch law firm. This meant he had to work sixty to seventy hours a week and commute almost two hours a day so that his family could live in the suburbs. On most weekends he had to bring work home. And on vacations he usually had to take his laptop so he could answer emails. When Meredith was ten, her dad had to rent an apartment in the city because the commuting was too exhausting for him. He only came home on weekends. He gave all three kids expensive college educations, cars, and extravagant weddings. At twenty-five, this is how Meredith describes their relationship: "I know dad loves me, but I can't imagine our talking about anything personal. To be honest, he doesn't know much about my life. He never really did. As a teenager, I felt he was intruding on our family since he only came home from the city on the weekends. I'm a lot closer to mom because she raised me."

Jeanette's parents took a different path. Her mother is a hairstylist and her dad is a high school teacher. Her mom worked full-time, including Saturdays. Dad spent more time with the kids since he had summers and Saturdays off. When Jeanette went to college, she had to take out loans to pay her way. When she married, she and her fiancé paid for the wedding because their parents couldn't afford it. This is how Jeanette describes her relationship with her dad: "I'm actually closer to him than to mom. I guess it's because we spent more time together while I was growing up. He got home about the same time I did after school. We'd cook dinner together before mom got home. I'd say he's one of my best friends." These two fathers and daughters love each other but each dad's job had a very different impact on his relationship with his daughter. So let's explore how dad's work has influenced your relationship.

Workaholic Dad. I can't tell you how many times I've heard daughters criticize their dad for being a workaholic. "He spent too much time at the job and not enough time with the family." I rarely meet a daughter who doesn't complain about a time when her dad couldn't make it to some special event because he had to work. What saddens and surprises me is that most of these daughters are angry or disappointed with dad instead of feeling sorry for him—or instead of admiring him. How can that be? Why do they feel anger instead of pity? Why disappointment instead of admiration? As Fran puts it: "Dad wasn't around enough while I was growing up. Mom did all the work of raising us. He seemed more interested in his job than in us. Making money is what mattered most to him. He didn't have to work seventy hours a week the way he did. Nobody forced him to. I guess family just wasn't that important to him."

Dad's Job: Burden or Blessing?

How did dad feel about himself and how did daughter feel about dad while the kids were growing up?

0 = never   1 = rarely
2 = fairly often   3 = almost always

Dad   Daughter

_____ _____ too focused on his job

_____ _____ too focused on making money

_____ _____ exhausted or grumpy when he got home

_____ _____ complained about the family not appreciating him enough

_____ _____ complained about the family spending too much money

_____ _____ uptight or tense about money or work

_____ _____ unhappy with his job

_____ _____ let the family down financially

_____ _____ enjoyed working more than being with family

_____ _____ enjoyed working as much as he did

_____ _____ **Your scores** (30 possible)

Given the importance our society places on making money, I'm stunned when daughters criticize their dads for having done what men are scripted or pressured to do: make lots of money. I ask daughters who feel like Fran to probe a little deeper: Isn't it possible that he loved your family so much that he sacrificed by doing whatever it took to earn as much money as he could for all of you? Why aren't you interpreting what he did as an act of love instead of a sign of not caring? Would you feel the same way if it was your mom who had worked this hard for your family? How do you know that nobody pressured your dad into working so hard? True, your dad wasn't physically "forced" into working seventy hours a week. But a man can certainly be emotionally pressured, emotionally forced, into doing a job he dislikes and into working far more hours—and far more years—than he wants. What makes you so sure that there weren't powerful emotions that "forced" your father into becoming a workaholic, such as being "forced" by the need to please his parents or by the desire to earn your mother's admiration? Step back. Think again. See if you can't put a brighter lens on this dark picture you have painted of your dad as a workaholic.

Materialistic Dad. Along the same lines, many daughters also tell me that their fathers are too materialistic. "He cares too much about having nice things." He's proud of what he has provided for the family: the big house, new cars, huge television, wine collection, membership at the club. Sometimes he even boasts about what he has accomplished. And that really irritates his daughter. As Melinda says: "I hate the way he's Mr. Show Off with the big house, all the wines, the fancy kitchen. He embarrasses me because he's always pointing out how much he spends on things. He seems so conceited because he makes way more money than his dad ever made." Again, what stuns me is that Melinda (and other daughters with her attitude) can't appreciate the sacrifices her dad has made—can't understand that when he brags or points out what he has spent, he is simply asking for what all of us want: love, admiration, appreciation. I wonder why these daughters haven't asked themselves: Does my dad think we love him or admire him for his money? Where might he have gotten that idea? Do mom, or we kids, or his parents *ever* seem really happy when he buys us nice things? Do any of us *ever* pay special attention to him when he takes us on those expensive vacations, or brings home the new car, or buys that really cool television? Is it any more materialistic for dad to buy fine wines or a fancy refrigerator than for us kids to want him to keep paying for our expensive vacations and our lavish weddings? Is dad really any more focused on money and expensive things than the rest of our family? Hmm.

Financial Losers. At the other extreme are daughters who complain that dad has let the family down by not making enough money. In his family's eyes, he's a financial "loser." Maybe he never lived up to his potential. Or maybe he has so little education and so few skills that he has never been able to support his family—or to support himself. Some daughters even blame dad because mom had to get a job, a job she doesn't like very much, either. If he'd made more money, mom could have stayed home. When daughters feel this way I suggest they do a little soul-searching. Would you feel so disappointed in your dad if he was a woman earning what he earns? Are you saying that a wife shouldn't ever have to shoulder any of the financial responsibility for the family, shouldn't have to lift some of that weight off her husband's back? Do you really know the reasons why your dad didn't succeed? If not, why not ask him rather than blame him?

Again, remember that being a "man" means being able to support your family—and to earn more money than your wife. So a man's self-confidence and self-esteem are largely based on his income.[29] This means that fathers who don't earn much money can end up feeling pretty bad about themselves. African American and Hispanic American fathers are especially hard hit on that front since they generally earn less than white fathers. While only 5 percent of white kids live in poverty, 35 percent of black kids and 25 percent of Hispanic American kids live in poverty. A black father is more likely than a white father to have a wife who earns more money than he does—17 percent versus 12 percent.[30] Not surprisingly, many low-income dads feel that their wives and daughters don't love or respect them.

Work Dad vs. Real Dad. Many daughters also get the wrong ideas about dad based on how he behaved when he got home from work. That is, they judge dad when he's at his worst, exhausted or preoccupied at the end of his workday. Without a chance to unwind—presto!—he's supposed to morph into Super Dad—the playful, laid-back, affectionate, energetic, talkative, attentive man who gives his kids all the attention they need. But it's not just how he treats his kids. *It's how he treats his wife.* His daughter is watching, and she's forming opinions about him—opinions that can last a lifetime. How does he treat mom? Does he seem happy to see her or does he complain about the messy house? Does he give her a hug or does he ask why dinner isn't ready? Does he talk to her during dinner or does he clam up and gobble down his food? Dads, your daughters were watching—and judging.

Daughters, think back to how you felt when your dad got home from work. How did he interact with you kids and with your mom? How would you describe him: playful, cheerful, peppy, loving, attentive, affectionate, laid-back, sweet, talkative, focused on the family—or uptight, grumpy, exhausted, distant, picky, preoccupied, bossy, touchy, critical, withdrawn, argumentative, spaced out? If your description is negative, are you able now to understand how his behavior was related to his job stress? To get a more accurate picture of your "real" dad versus your "work" dad, think about the times when he was happy and relaxed—vacations, parties, weekends. Replay those memories. Imagine that your father hadn't had such a stressful job, or such a long commute, or such a long day. Try to separate who your dad is as a person from who he was at the end of a workday while you were growing up. Think of it this way: How would you feel if the people you loved were judging you—and forming lifelong opinions about you—based on how you act during your worst weeks at school or when you get home from a bad day at work?

Dads, talk to your daughters about how you felt when you got home from work. Tell her what you wish you had done better—not just toward her, but toward her mother. Spend a few hours talking about the questions in the "Jobs and Money" questions below.

Jobs and Money: Questions for Dad

1. When you were young, what did you hope for in terms of work and money?
2. What people influenced the type of work you chose?
3. If money hadn't mattered at all, what kind of work would you have chosen?
4. What have you liked least and most about your work?
5. What advice would you give me about work, money, and happiness?
6. How well does your job fit your personality?

[125]

7. How has your work affected your family life?

8. When I was growing up, how did you usually feel when you got home from work?

9. What do you wish had been different about your job when I was young?

10. Do you think your dad is proud of you?

11. How do you define success, and how successful do you think you are?

12. What are the biggest mistakes you've made related to work or money?

13. If you could retire soon, what would you do afterwards?

14. What have you been proudest of in your work?

15. How much pleasure has your work given you over the years?

16. How would you feel if your wife earned more than you?

17. How would you feel about my marrying a man who earns much less than I do?

18. What have you lost or had to give up over the years because of your work?

19. How do you feel about the kind of work your father did?

20. What have people misunderstood about you in terms of your job or money?

After your talk, I bet many of these daughters' comments will sound familiar:

> **Meg:** *"My dad told me that if he could do it all again, he wouldn't work for a big corporation and make all this money. All these years I thought he loved his work and that it was just normal for dads never to be at home. I didn't re-*

alize it bothered him to be away from me so much. As successful and well known as he is, I'm stunned."

Dawn: "I understood why he didn't like it that my mom made more money than him. Now I see that he wasn't being jealous or competitive or mean to her. He just felt like a loser."

Rachel: "I had never thought about what it was like for him to commute two hours to work for twenty-three years to a job he hated. I almost feel guilty for having lived such a rich life while he worked his butt off for all of us."

Mary Lynn: "I didn't like the way he was so obsessed with money. And he'd get upset with mom for spending too much. She'd laugh and brush him off. So we three girls never took him seriously. After he told me about his poor childhood, I felt a pang of guilt thinking about how selfish the four of us must have seemed to him."

Money Matters

- Adults with a graduate or professional degree earn an average of $80,000 compared to $20,000 for those without a high school diploma.
- Almost one third of adults graduate from college.
- Women are almost as likely as men to graduate from high school and college.
- About 20 percent of wives are more educated and earn more money than their husbands.
- Most parents can't afford to retire at sixty-five.
- American parents have loaned their adult kids about 68 billion dollars—loans that many have no intention of repaying.[31]

[127]

- Families earning more than $62,000 spend roughly $250,000 to raise each child, *not including* college expenses.[32]
- Many young adults have gotten used to a lifestyle on dad's money that they can't afford on their own incomes.[33]

College Years: Banking on Dad

After a daughter finishes high school, money tends to create more tension between her and her dad. Why? Partly because college expenses come into play: Who is going to pay for what? How much will dad pay? How much will daughter pay? What's reasonable for her to spend each month? And if she isn't going to college, how much is dad supposed to help her out financially? If she has a job and lives at home, how much is she going to chip in for food and rent? At what point is dad going to stop giving her money? When is she going to be self-reliant? After college graduation? After graduate school? After she's married? After she turns thirty? Never?

If you two haven't already resolved these matters, it's time. You need to have some long talks about the questions in the "Banking on Dad" quiz. Daughters, be sure you have your facts straight. Study the "Money Matters" section on page 127. Memorize these facts. Keep these financial realities front and center when talking to your dad.

The higher your score on the "Banking on Dad" quiz, the more the daughter is still relying on dad to help her out financially. Most dads want their adult daughters to be financially self-reliant—the sooner, the better. But some dads enjoy being their daughter's banker as much as she enjoys being daddy's little girl who relies on his money. If this is the arrangement the two of you make, just remember the

Banking on Dad?

How do each of you feel about these matters?

0 = absolutely not   1 = maybe
2 = probably   3 = definitely

After I graduate from high school, dad should:

Dad   Daughter

_____   _____ Continue to pay all my educational and living expenses.

_____   _____ Loan me money instead of telling me to get a bank loan.

_____   _____ Pay for my graduate school education, or part of it.

_____   _____ Pay for most (or all) of my wedding.

_____   _____ Set aside some money for me as an inheritance.

_____   _____ Let me live at home for free after I've finished school and have a job.

_____   _____ Help me make a down payment on a house.

_____   _____ Pay for most (or all) of my first car.

_____   _____ Pay for my health and car insurance until I finish my education.

_____   _____ Offer to give me money whenever I need it.

_____   _____ **Your scores** (30 possible)

Golden Rule: He who has the gold, makes the rules. When a daughter accepts the "gold" from her dad, it can—and often does—complicate the relationship. *Both* of you need to consider how much of a say dad is going to have in his daughter's decisions as long as he is still bankrolling her. Where will you draw the line? How much of dad's money is on the line? What price will he pay later in terms of retiring or being free to work less? Why does dad keep handing over the money? Is he insecure about how much his daughter loves him? Is he trying to make up for something he thinks he hasn't given her? Even if he is rich enough to keep helping her for the rest of his life, is that in her best interest—or in your relationship's best interest?

I can't tell you what financial arrangement is best for you. But I can tell you to be up-front with each other. Make your arrangement clear. Daughters, just keep in mind that if you want your dad to stop treating you like a little girl, you have to behave like an adult financially. As women, how can we expect our fathers to treat us like grown-ups if we still have our hands out for money? How can we expect our dads to re-spect our judgment if we're still dependent on them finan-cially? At what age will we stop asking, expecting, or *allowing* our fathers to be our instant cash machines? If we choose to keep accepting his money, are we prepared to accept the ten-sions that go along with that deal?

Dads, keep these thoughts in mind. Even though you love your daughter, you don't have to prove your love with money. You can be a very loving dad and still say "Enough. You're on your own." Getting your daughter to stand on her own two feet isn't mean or cold-hearted. Just because you can afford to keep helping her out doesn't necessarily mean that is the wise thing to do.

Daughter's Career Plans

Finally, a daughter's career plans (or lack of!) can create tension between her and her father. Some daughters feel that dad is disappointed and doesn't approve of what's she's done—or what she's planning to do. She hasn't measured up to his expectations—or so she thinks. He's disappointed because she's not successful enough—or so she fears. If dad is a big success, she's afraid she won't ever be able to match him, and if he isn't very successful, she feels she has to be a superstar to make him proud. Sometimes a daughter feels uncomfortable around dad because she has screwed up in terms of preparing for a job or finding one. And everyone in the family knows it. As Harriet said, "I didn't study hard while I was in school. I played around too much. Now I'm not going to be able to get the best job. Honestly, I have no idea what I want to do when I graduate. I dread telling dad because he's spent so much money on my education. I'm sure everyone in the family sees me as the black sheep—the loser."

Dads, when you see your daughter flopping around and making stupid decisions, or on the verge of making one, what are you supposed to do? Here's what I bet you usually do: You jump right in and start offering her advice on how to make things better. You mean well. You love her. You want to help her before she makes an even bigger mess of things. And then what happens? She gets mad at you—defensive, angry, emotional. She says you're criticizing her. She feels put down. She verbally attacks you: "You don't care how I feel. You're always pressuring me. Can't you see I'm doing the best I can? Get off my back! Stop treating me like a child. Stop being so critical. You're stressing me out!"

What's a dad to do? Well, here's what *not* to do: Don't jump in and start giving your daughter advice. Instead, approach her when she's in a good mood. Ask if the two of you can go to lunch somewhere or go for a long walk. Tell her you've noticed that she's been stressed and unhappy lately about work stuff or about what she's going to do when she graduates. Ask her if she would like to talk to you about this. Tell her you'd like to talk about those times when you were her age and felt confused or insecure about work or school. Tell her you'd like to "share" some of the things you learned the hard way from your own mistakes. "Sharing" is different from giving advice because you're talking about yourself and your mistakes. If she says no, then tell her anytime she changes her mind, you're there for her. Say no more. Just wait.

Daughters, if you are stressed by job issues, my guess is you're taking it out on your dad. When he tries to help by offering advice, you snap at him. You reject him. You criticize him. You interpret everything he says as a criticism instead of as a gift he's trying to give you. You act like a child instead of allowing him to have an adult conversation with you. Why are you treating him like this? Because you don't feel very good about yourself right now—the confusion, uncertainty, and stress about what lies ahead—or because you feel stupid for some of the choices you've made, such as not working hard enough to prepare for a good job, not planning well for your future, or not saving enough money.

Why not try this instead? When you're feeling calm, tell your dad that you want his feedback on ways to improve your job and money situation. Tell him that you're nervous talking about this because you aren't feeling too good about yourself right now. Ask him to start off by telling you stories about mistakes he made when he was younger. Ask him to tell you about times he felt confused or stressed about starting a career. If you start feeling criticized, tell him. Ask him for a hug. See

[132]

him as your ally, not your enemy. Think of your conversation as a brainstorming session where two friends are working toward a common goal—and that goal is helping you, the daughter he loves. Above all, remember that many successful daughters look back later in life and give their dads credit for how far they have gotten in their careers. Take heart!

Dad's Influence: Daughter's Success[34]

Hillary Clinton, senator and presidential candidate, praises her father, Hugh Rodham, who ran a drapery fabric business in Chicago. *"I recently reread letters he wrote to me when I was at Wellesley and Yale, usually in response to a despondent collect call home in which I expressed doubts about my abilities or confusion about where my life was heading. I doubt anyone meeting my father or being on the receiving end of his caustic criticism would ever have imagined the tender love and advice he offered to buck me up, straighten me out, and keep me going."*

Condoleezza Rice, first African American female secretary of state, says her father, Reverend John Rice, was a hugely influential person in her life. *"I have become convinced over the years that there is no more important relationship for a girl than the one she has with her father. More than anything, my father was always my friend. He was my confidant and my counselor, the person I turned to first when I wanted to share some good news or needed to work through some bad times."*

Dianne Feinstein, California senator, is grateful to her father, Leon Goldman, for his impact on her career. *"My father was a fine surgeon, a careful scholar, and a great teacher. He was a loyal friend and a proud father. I miss him deeply every* day. And when I see the power of compassion or hard work prove out, I think of my father and know that he would look on and smile."

Barbara Mandrell, country music legend and award-winning singer, had her father, Irby, as her business manager for thirty-eight years. *"Times were pretty tough when I first started recording and touring and it was Daddy who made hangin' in there possible for me. In those days, Daddy was not only my manager, but he also booked my dates, played rhythm guitar, and sang backup in my band."*

Rosanne Cash, Grammy-winning singer and song-writer, and her father Johnny Cash, one of the most famous musicians in America, had a strong bond even in the last days of his life. *"Not a day goes by that I don't think of him, or think of something I would like to share with him, or long for his advice, which I didn't ask for nearly often enough."*

Anne Graham Lotz, daughter of evangelist Billy Graham and CEO of Angel Ministries, followed in his career footsteps. She recalled what her father said when she was a teenager after she wrecked her parents' car. *"'Anne, I knew all along about your wreck. I was just waiting for you to tell me. I love you. We can fix the car. You're going to be a better driver because of this.' At that moment I realized what an incredibly wonderful father I had."*

Mothers:
Father Friendly or Not? 6

❖

- *When I'm upset with dad, I get mom to talk to him for me. What's wrong with that?*
- *My daughter won't talk to me when she's upset without going to mom first. That hurts my feelings.*
- *Mom's feelings would be hurt if I did things with dad without including her. Can you blame her?*
- *When I want time alone with my daughter, it's like I'm intruding on the mother-daughter thing.*
- *Mom has sacrificed more than dad for us kids. So of course we're closer to her.*
- *It's just natural for a daughter to be closer to her mom than to her dad because they're both women.*
- *Mom would be jealous if I went to dad with personal things instead of going to her.*
- *I feel like my wife's sidekick because she says she knows more about how to raise a girl than I do.*

You're probably not surprised by these comments, are you? In our own families most of us see that daughters generally are closer to and more involved with their mothers than their fathers. Throughout their lifetimes, mother and daughter usually get to know each other better and talk about more personal things than father and daughter.[1-5] But does it have to be this way? If your relationship is in second place compared to mom's, how did this happen? And what can you do about it now?

Idealizing Mothers

For daughters, fathers often come in second to mothers in part because our society idealizes mothers—and often denigrates fathers. From media to children's storybooks, moms usually come across as more unselfish, understanding, sympathetic, insightful, trustworthy, and self-sacrificing than dads. For example, several Verizon commercials were taken off the air because viewers complained that the father was portrayed in such a negative way.[6] And in award-winning children's books from 1938–2002, dads interact far less than moms with their kids.[7] Many commercials, sitcoms, Father's Day cards, and comic strips also make dad look like a moron compared to mom.[8-11] The same is true for most Hollywood movies with their negligent, blundering dads and devoted supermoms.[12-14]

We also idealize mothers by exaggerating the differences between the ways that men and women communicate and interact with their kids—with mom being superior. In reality, moms and dads are more similar than different when it comes to nurturing, communicating, and parenting.[15, 16] As for the uglier side of motherhood, we often ignore or downplay the realities. For example, 906,000 children are abused or neglected every year—and 1,500 of them die, most under the age of four. More than 40 percent of these children are neglected or abused by their mothers acting alone, 18 percent by their fathers alone, and 17 percent by parents together.[17] There are also mothers who sexually abuse their sons and daughters for years—a reality rarely discussed in the media.[18] Despite our idealized belief that all women "instinctively" and blissfully embrace motherhood, not all automatically or comfortably bond with their newborns.[19, 20]

Idealizing someone isn't the same as admiring, loving, or respecting him or her. Idealizing someone is an unhealthy situation where you deny reality, create illusions, and lie to yourself about your idol. So how do you know if you are idealizing your mother—or your father? First, you get extremely angry at anyone who points out your idol's flaws, even if that person is a therapist or a family member. You can't stand thinking about the things you suspect (or know) this person has done wrong. You want everyone to believe your idol is superior to the rest of us. The things you remember your idol doing in the past are almost always good memories. If your idol does make a mistake, you find a way to excuse it—often by blaming your other parent.

As children we idealize our parents. Idealizing them makes us feel safe and secure. And that's good. But as we age, our parents need to make sure we outgrow these childish beliefs so that we see them realistically as *imperfect* people. Dad needs to let his daughter know that he is not a Prince Charming, not a knight in shining armor. He needs to allow her to see that he is sometimes weak, confused, frightened, fragile, vulnerable, dependent. And mom needs to do the same to be sure the kids don't put her on a pedestal as "mother superior."

If you idealized your mom while you were growing up (or maybe still do), how much impact does that have on you and your dad? Lots! To begin with, you probably *still* side with her against him. You see her point of view before you see his. You feel she is right far more often than he is. You see your dad through her eyes, not through your own. For instance, Pat's mom has always thought her husband was stingy and too worried about money. But instead of finding out why her dad might be worried about money, Pat automatically assumes mom is right, and dad is painfully aware that both women make snide remarks about his being a penny pincher. They not only ridicule him to his face, they gripe to each other behind his back—especially when they're out together on a shopping spree. Feeling that the two women gang up against him, he sadly gives up and slowly backs away from Pat. After all, she's already made up her mind about him just like his wife has.

Then too, if you idealize one parent, you wind up demonizing the other parent. Needing to believe that mom is far more perfect than everyone else, you blame her shortcomings or her mistakes on someone else—namely, your dad. Almost anyone can be picked as the bad guy, as long as it's not your mother. You may be overly critical of dad because you're trying to preserve your image of your mother as the saint, the martyr, the fragile victim. And since you don't feel comfortable getting angry at your idol, when you are frustrated or upset with her you take it out on dad. For instance, if you discover that your mom cheated on your dad, you might tell yourself, "If dad had been a better husband, mom wouldn't have had that affair. She was just lonely because dad didn't spend enough time with her. Besides, mom didn't leave the marriage. She was such a fine person that she quit seeing the guy after dad found out."

Father-Friendly Mothers

A father-friendly mom doesn't allow her kids to idealize her. By "father friendly," I mean mothers whose beliefs and behavior strengthen children's bonds with their fathers. From the time the kids are born, the father-friendly mom actively and enthusiastically shares the parenting, allowing and encouraging dad to be equally involved. Instead of criticizing, supervising, or correcting the way he interacts with the kids, she compliments and appreciates him. And the kids see this, day after day, year after year. This mom isn't rolling her eyes, arching her eyebrows, or making disapproving faces that let the kids know she thinks dad is an idiot—an unwanted intruder, a rookie player on *her* parenting field. She rarely criticizes or ridicules him as a parent; if she does, it's not in front of the kids. She doesn't act like she's the child-rearing expert and dad is her inferior sidekick or her slow-witted student. She makes her husband feel valued and confident as a parent. She doesn't give the kids the impression that she is more self-sacrificing, more dedicated, or more loving than their dad. In short, she believes her husband is just as good a parent as she is—and the kids know it.

When it comes to discipline, dad isn't the bad cop who deals out most of the punishment. She doesn't say, "Just wait until your father gets home!" Instead, she confidently stands up to the kids and exerts her authority without making her husband do all the dirty work as disciplinarian. Showing the kids that they can't push her around, she strengthens their bonds with dad because the kids won't see him as the judgmental, strict, or unsympathetic parent. And she doesn't align herself with the kids against their father. For example, she doesn't undermine dad by saying, "Let's not let your father find out what you did because he will be get mad at you. I

Father-Friendly Moms

Dad: How did your daughter's mother feel about you when the kids were younger?

Daughter: How did your mom feel about your dad while you kids were growing up?

0 = never, rarely 1 = most of the time 2 = almost always

Dad Daughter

_____ _____ Your father is just as loving and nurturing as I am.

_____ _____ I want you to talk to dad about personal things.

_____ _____ Your dad has sacrificed as much as I have for you kids.

_____ _____ You and your dad need to be just as close as we are.

_____ _____ Your dad knows just as much as I do about raising you.

_____ _____ Your father is just as sympathetic as I am.

_____ _____ You and dad need to spend just as much time alone as we do.

_____ _____ You ought to have private conversations with your dad without me around.

_____ _____ Your father's way of disciplining you is just as good as mine.

_____ _____ Your father enjoys being a parent as much as I do.

_____ _____ **Your scores** (20 possible)

[140]

won't tell him what you did. It will just be our little secret."
She doesn't send the anti-father message that she is the accepting and forgiving parent, but dad is the judgmental, tough
guy.

As father and daughter, use the "Father-Friendly Moms"
quiz to start examining the ways in which mom has influenced your father-daughter relationship. Mom's attitudes
about the kind of relationship a daughter should have with
her mother and with her father play a crucial role in the
shaping the kind of relationships that develop within the
family over the years.

The higher your scores, the easier it was for dad and
daughter to create just as close a relationship as mom and
daughter have. Mom's positive feelings build dad's confidence
as a parent and allow him to be *equally* involved in the kids'
lives. Mom's positive feelings also help a daughter focus on
dad's strengths instead of on his weaknesses as a parent. Her
husband isn't likely to feel like Marcus does: "My wife criticizes, mocks, and disagrees with me about the way to raise our
daughter. I end up looking like an idiot in front of my daughter. So I've just given up. It's easier to keep quiet and let her
do things her way."

Generally speaking, father-friendly mothers have several
things in common.[21,22] They had a joyful, loving relationship
with their fathers while they were growing up. These women
value and appreciate men as parents, instead of looking down
on men or feeling that fathers aren't as necessary as moms.
These moms usually work full-time outside the home once
their children start school. This means they're less likely than
stay-at-home moms to become overly dependent or overly involved with their kids. Given her background and her interests outside the family, her kids see her as a "glad mom," not a

Sad Mom or Glad Mom?

For most of your childhood, how would you describe your mother?

0 = never   I = sometimes   2 = quite a bit
3 = often/almost always

_____ upbeat and content

_____ self-reliant and independent

_____ having interests aside from being a mother

_____ self-confident

_____ working at a job she liked

_____ happy in her marriage

_____ free from depression

_____ happy with her relationship with her dad

_____ satisfied with herself

_____ emotionally sturdy and resilient

_____ **Score** (30 possible)

"sad mom." And that's good news because these self-reliant, contented wives allow and encourage their husbands to build the strongest bonds with their kids. As father and daughter, use the "Sad Mom or Glad Mom?" quiz to discuss mom's impact on your relationship.

The higher the score, the more secure and confident your mother felt. She could back off and let her husband bond with the kids. She didn't always have to be number one or center stage in her daughter's eyes. Dad could have that place of honor too. Sadly, not all mothers are father friendly, in large part because of their troubled or distant relationships with their fathers. So let's see what impact these mothers have on dads and daughters:

1) the sacrificing martyr mom
2) the jealous, competitive mom
3) the unhappily married mom[23, 24]

Dad as Couch Potato?

- 80 percent of dads earn most of the money for the family—of those, 20 percent earn all of it.[25]
- Counting housework, childcare, and paid work, most mothers only work forty-one hours a week while most fathers work fifty-one hours.[26]
- Dads are spending more time than ever with their kids, roughly 20 percent less than moms when the mom works outside the home.[27, 28]
- Today's moms and dads work longer hours outside the home, do less housework, and spend more time with their kids than parents in years past.[29]
- Younger men are more likely than older men to say they would give up some of their income to spend more time with their kids.[30]

The Sacrificing Martyr Mom

In your family, did everyone feel that dad was doing his fair share of the childcare and work at home? Or did anyone feel that mom was sacrificing more for the kids than dad was? Did anyone think mom was the unselfish martyr and dad was the selfish ruler? If so, you kids probably felt sorry for mom and irritated with dad because you thought he was taking advantage of her. Sure, there are husbands who slack off at home, dumping too much work on their wives. But that is *not* how most men in our country behave, as you can see from the statistics in the "Dad as Couch Potato?" section on page 143. So why do some daughters still get the idea that dad's a slouch and mom's a martyr. How can that happen?

To begin with, a lot of the work that men do at home goes unnoticed. Kids notice the things that most mothers do at home: cooking, cleaning, washing clothes, vacuuming, grocery shopping, taking kids to the doctor, and driving kids around. Her work is visible to children. But many men do things at home that kids don't notice: repairing, assembling, installing, cleaning, and maintaining computers, tools, appliances, cars, toys, pools, outdoor lighting, barbeque grills; doing yard work; shoveling snow; cleaning gutters; moving furniture; repairing the roof; doing the bookkeeping and financial planning (health and car insurance, taxes, investments); replacing heat and air conditioning filters; cleaning basements and attics; building fires; rewiring; unplugging drains.

Take Joel, for instance. He spends time at night after the kids are in bed taking care of the family finances: reading about investments, health plans, and college savings programs, keeping things in order for tax returns, paying bills, and so on, none of which his kids "see" the way they do when mom cooks dinner. Kids may appreciate and thank mom, "Great dinner!" but they are less likely to appreciate or thank dad, "Great tax return and super-clean gutters. Thanks, dad!"

Remember that the media floods us with the idea that moms continue working frantically after they get home from their jobs while lazy dads chill out in front of the television.

That's why the father-friendly mom makes clear to the kids that their dad is no slouch and she's no martyr.

The Jealous Mom

Do either of you ever feel that mom gets jealous if the two of you spend too much time together or talk about personal things without including her? For instance, how would your mom (or your wife) feel if you phoned and asked to speak to your dad—and you asked her to get off the phone? Would she be all right if you were talking sports, money, or school stuff—but not all right if you were talking about your boyfriend, trouble with your roommate, or other "personal" stuff? How would your mom feel if you and your dad went off for a weekend, or if dad visited you and your husband without taking mom along? If you two never do these kinds of things together, why not? Mom and daughter do, right? So why not dad and daughter? Is it because mom would get jealous?

As Burt, a fifty-year-old father, explains: "Even when Jessica was a little girl, I could tell that my wife got jealous when she thought I was intruding on her mother-daughter thing. She just wasn't comfortable when Jess wanted to be with me as much as with her. She'd get very competitive, like we were in some kind of contest for Jess's love. When Jessica became a teenager, my wife told me it wasn't right for me to spend time alone with her. So I backed off. I didn't want my wife upset with me all the time."

Unfortunately a jealous mom has a lasting impact on her daughter's bond with her dad, as these daughters explain:

"If I asked to talk to dad on the phone, my mom would automatically think I wanted to talk about money. She'd be really hurt when she found out it was something personal.

She'd feel replaced and her self-worth would be diminished."

"No way! My mother loves the position she holds— the one who has to know everything that's going on in the family. She always has to be on the phone or in the room."

"When dad and I are trying to talk, mom literally talks over him—almost like he doesn't exist. I couldn't get as close to him as I want because it would reinforce her insecurity about not having a career."

"Mom would die if I ever talked to dad about my boyfriend instead of talking to her. She would never say anything directly to me, but she'd let me know I had hurt her. I have never shared much with dad because I don't want to hurt mom."

As for spending a few days with dad without including mom, many daughters would never consider such a thing as these comments attest:

"I couldn't do it because mom has always wanted me to feel closer to her and need her most."

"Now that she works two days a week, my dad takes off from work early so we can spend time alone without upsetting her. But that's as far as we can go."

"When I tell her that dad and I are getting closer, I get the feeling she thinks my relationship with him is just fine the way it is. I don't think she'd like our spending a weekend alone."

"You've got to be kidding! My mom is already jealous just because I'm taking your Fathers and Daughters course. And she'd find some way to make dad feel guilty."

Happily Married—or Not!

While you were growing up, were your parents happy together? Did your mom think your dad was a great husband—
and did she let you know it? As a dad, did you feel your wife let
the kids know that you were quite a catch—a lucky catch for
her? Let's hope so, because an unhappy marriage damages many
father-daughter relationships. Most marriages go through tough
times, especially in the year after a couple's first baby is born.[31]
And most parents argue sometimes—usually about their kids,
money, sex, and housework.[32] That's not what matters to the
kids. What matters is the overall quality of the marriage—
above all how mom feels about dad as a husband. The "Dad as
a Husband: Through Mom's Eyes" quiz on page 148 can help
you answer that crucial question. Use the quiz as an opportunity
to talk about how mom's feelings have affected your father-
daughter relationship.

Why are we focusing on mom's happiness—or unhappiness—instead of dad's? Because in most marriages the wife is
more dissatisfied with the marriage than the husband. In fact,
many husbands aren't aware that their wives are unhappy—
many men are shocked when a wife announces she wants a divorce.[33] Given this, a daughter is probably going to be affected
by her mom's unhappiness before she's affected by her dad's.
And that's why it's important to figure out how your mom's
feelings about her marriage affected your father-daughter relationship (hopefully in more good ways than bad).

First, unhappily married moms usually start spending
much more time with the kids, becoming more dependent on
them and shutting dad out. Often the daughter becomes her
mother's confidante, protector, defender, and advisor. She gets
pulled into her parents' marriage in ways that make her think less
of her dad. With mom pointing out dad's flaws, the daughter not

Dad as a Husband: Through Mom's Eyes

Dad: What did you think your wife felt about you as a husband while the kids were growing up?

Daughter: What did you think your mother felt about your dad while you kids were growing up?

0 = rarely   1 = half the time   2 = almost always

Dad Daughter

Dad	Daughter	
_____	_____	loving
_____	_____	communicative
_____	_____	thoughtful, considerate
_____	_____	attentive
_____	_____	playful
_____	_____	appreciative, complimentary
_____	_____	loyal/trustworthy
_____	_____	comforting/nurturing
_____	_____	forgiving
_____	_____	nonjudgmental/accepting
_____	_____	unselfish/giving
_____	_____	generous
_____	_____	fair/reasonable
_____	_____	sympathetic/understanding
_____	_____	supportive/encouraging
_____	_____	**Your scores** (30 possible)

only feels sorry for her mother, she views dad through her mother's eyes—and it's not a pretty view! With mom criticizing dad, daughter slowly withdraws from him emotionally. Mother and daughter become more like best friends or sisters than parent and child, aligned together against dad. Needless to say, these daughters are angry and disappointed in dad. After all, he's responsible for mom's misery.

Second, the daughter becomes so overly involved in her mother's life that they become like one person. They become *enmeshed*. Yes, dads and daughters sometimes become enmeshed, but not nearly as often as mothers and daughters. So how do you know if you're enmeshed? Here are some danger signs: You absorb whatever negative beliefs and feelings your mother has about your father. You treat him like she does, belittling or criticizing him, ignoring or avoiding him, demeaning or nagging at him. You feel responsible for making mom happy. You feel you have to stand up for her—to protect her from dad, not from physical violence, but just to be on her side emotionally. You have allowed yourself to be put in the middle of their marriage. You might even feel guilty about the thought of moving too far away from her because she needs you so much. It's almost as if you've become *her* parent, which is why psychologists say there is a "role reversal." The higher a daughter's score on the "Are You Enmeshed with Mom?" quiz on page 150, the more likely it is that the father-daughter relationship has been damaged. As a dad, how enmeshed do you think your daughter was—or is—with her mom? As a daughter, do you agree or disagree with him?

Third, if mom isn't happy in the marriage, dad usually withdraws more from his daughter. He knows that you and your mother are talking about him behind his back and he knows that what you're hearing about him isn't good. It's two

QUIZ

Are You Enmeshed with Mom?

Dad: As your daughter was growing up, how do you think she felt about her mother?

Daughter: As you were growing up, how did you feel about your mother?

0 = Never 1 = rarely 2 = fairly often 4 = almost always

Dad   Daughter

_____ _____ I have a hard time saying no to her.

_____ _____ I feel it's my responsibility to make her happier.

_____ _____ I can't enjoy my own happiness when she's unhappy.

_____ _____ I feel it's my responsibility to help her solve problems in her life.

_____ _____ I feel selfish or guilty when I ask her to give up something for me.

_____ _____ I give up doing things in order to make her happy.

_____ _____ I feel like her counselor, advisor, or best friend.

_____ _____ I see her as really lonely or sad.

_____ _____ I worry about what's going to happen to her.

_____ _____ I feel she needs me as much or more than she needs her husband.

_____ _____ **Your scores** (40 possible)

against one. What's he supposed to do? He thinks he's losing your love. He knows his wife isn't happy with him. Should he try to talk to you about what's going on? Hurt and confused, he backs away, which is just one more flaw you can hold against him.

Many daughters know that things are going downhill with dad. But they don't know what to do about it:

> "Mom points out his flaws in front of me. It makes me and my father uncomfortable around each other."
>
> "My mom is constantly putting him down for small things she doesn't like about him. I have taken on a nagging tone with him too. I know he hates the way we talk to him like he's a child."
>
> "I wish she would stop telling me about their fights. But when I tell her I don't want to hear it, she says I don't care about her. She says I am taking his side when I tell her to leave me out of their crap."
>
> "The hostile things she tells me about dad stick in my mind for much longer than a few hours. I take to heart everything she says and find myself resenting my dad."
>
> "My mom doesn't have many friends. She has always told me and my sister about her arguments with dad. She's even asked us if we think she should leave him. It makes it very difficult to see him from my own perspective."

Fourth, adultery is more common in unhappy marriages. Chances are if dad cheats, his relationship with his daughter is going to be damaged far more than if mom cheats. Why? In part it's because the media encourage us to react more harshly to a father's infidelity than to a mother's. As we've already discussed, the media's messages do have an impact on our attitudes and our reactions to other people. So what do we learn about adultery from most movies, television shows, and magazine articles? Just this: If mom cheats, it's because dad is a lousy husband. We sympathize with her because she is searching for someone to love—not for sexual pleasure or selfish amusement. Besides, the man she cheats with is a pretty good guy, not a young, sexy, empty-headed, gold-digging playboy. We want to forgive mom for her "mistake" because she is still a wonderful parent. But when dad cheats, whoa! Dad isn't a lonely husband who falls in love with another woman because his wife ignores, demeans, or mistreats him. He's a self-centered fool who's only after sex—meaningless, loveless sex. And how about the woman he cheats with? You guessed it—she's a young, gorgeous gal who is after his money, doesn't mind breaking up his marriage, and isn't really in love with him. Is it any wonder that a daughter may react more harshly to dad's infidelity than to mom's?

When a daughter tells me how upset she is at dad for cheating, I first ask her: Are you treating your father the same way you would treat your mother if she cheated? Can you possibly accept that his affair had more to do with loneliness than with sex? Are you making the worst assumptions about him before checking out the facts? Then I ask: Why do you feel that your father betrayed *you*? Why do you say that *you* can't trust him anymore? Why do you feel it's *you* who has to forgive him? Yes, adultery is a betrayal. And yes, it is breaking a trust, breaking a promise—the promise not to make love to anyone except your spouse. But the betrayal and the broken promise is between husband and wife—not between parent and child. Your father has broken a promise he made to your mother, not a promise he made to you. He has not done anything to you that would cause you not to trust him as a parent. I'm not saying you won't feel hurt, angry, or deeply disap-

[152]

pointed. I'm saying that it's not your place to punish him, to forgive him, or to decide how to repair the trust. That's up to your mother, not to you.

Think about it this way: If your mother has been a pretty darn good parent all these years, if she has been trustworthy with you, why would you suddenly decide she didn't deserve your trust—or decide you don't love her as much—if she cheats on your dad? If you and she have a good relationship, why would you choose to damage that relationship by punishing her for cheating on your dad? Yes, your dad is going to have to figure out how—or if—he can forgive her. And time will tell if he can ever trust your mom again. But it's not your issue—*it's theirs.*

Let's learn from Louise, who finally understood how her parents' miserable marriage had nearly destroyed her relationship with her dad:

> *"When I was growing up, I could see that my parents weren't happy together. They were always arguing. And my dad had such a temper. Mom would get home from work and fix dinner. As soon as she heard dad's key in the lock, she'd look at us with disgust and say, 'Here comes the dictator.' He'd want to eat in a big hurry. And then he'd criticize her cooking. They'd both start yelling. My brother and I would leave the table and go to our rooms. The way I saw it, my dad was the bad guy. Why did he always have to complain about her food? Why did he have to be so grouchy when he got home? Why did he usually seem so angry at her? I sided with my mom, which would make him even madder. And I felt he loved my brother more than me because he would side with dad. Then everything changed. When I was twenty-eight my mom told me that she had*

been having an affair for many years and that she was thinking of divorcing dad and marrying this wealthy man. Dad had known about the other man all those years, yet he never left her. Suddenly I realized why he had been so angry all the time. His wife didn't love him. But for the sake of us kids he stuck with her, knowing that she was in love with this rich man. It must have been torture for him. He wasn't yelling about her cooking, he was really screaming at what she was doing to him. Anyway, from that time on, I changed towards my father. I started taking his side— which infuriated my mother. I started reaching out to him, spending time with him, listening to him. Years later when he died, we were much closer than he and my brother ever were. To this day, I miss him. And to this day I feel sad for all the pain he endured."

Strengthening Your Bond

If some of mom's attitudes and behavior over the years have limited or damaged your father-daughter relationship, what can you do about it now? First, you can start spending a lot more time with each other without mom around. We've talked about why this is so important in an earlier chapter. Both of you need to commit to this together. Chances are your mom isn't going to be overjoyed with this new arrangement. So as a husband and as a daughter, you both need to reassure mom that the reason you're spending more time together without her has nothing to do with her being a failure in any way. Just let her know that you two want to get to know each other better—which means spending more time together.

As a daughter, if your mother criticizes your father or if she confides in you about their marital problems, tell her to stop. Without getting angry, let her know that you aren't going to be her advisor or her confidante any longer. In a calm voice tell her that if she's unhappy with your dad, she should talk to a counselor, her rabbi or minister, or a friend. Let her know that when she says negative things to you about your dad, she is making *you* tense and uncomfortable. Focus on how *she* is hurting *you*, how *she* is stressing you out. Don't focus on how she is hurting your relationship with your dad. Tell her that you're not taking his side—or her side. Tell her that you're getting a divorce—you're divorcing yourself from their marriage—with or without her blessing. You don't need her approval or her permission to release you from being part of their marriage.

Divorce and Remarriage: Resolving, Renewing, Repairing

7

❖

- *My daughter has pushed me away ever since the divorce. No matter how hard I try, she's not very interested in being with me. I feel like her mother is turning her against me. Even though I've paid all my child support, my daughter thinks I'm stingy and selfish. I feel there's nothing left to do but leave her alone. She treats me like her mom was the only one who raised her. Why can't she see how much I've been hurt?*

- *Things have been strained with dad. I think he cares more about his girlfriend than about me. I get the feeling I don't matter that much anymore. Besides that, I worry when I'm with him that he might say something bad about mom—or that he'll want to talk about their divorce.*

- *After the divorce, things just sort of fell apart between us as time passed. I'm not even sure why exactly. Now it just seems like there's no way to reconnect. I don't even know what the first step would be—or who should make the first move. It's been so long.*

Sound familiar? After parents divorce, most fathers and daughters experience these kinds of stress and separation. It may not make you feel better, but at least you're not alone. Nearly one third of the daughters in our country have parents who are divorced.

America's Families

Who are children under the age of eighteen living with?[1]

55%	mother and father—4 percent unmarried
11%	single mother, never married
12%	single mother, divorced
14%	mother and stepfather
5%	neither parent
2%	mother and her boyfriend
1%	single father, never married
1%	single father, divorced
1%	father and stepmother
.5%	father and his girlfriend

Who Pays the Price?

So what? Most daughters adjust to their parents' divorce without long-term damage, right? Well, yes—and no. Yes, most daughters do become well-adjusted, successful adults even though their parents are divorced. But most daughters' relationships with their fathers are damaged—sometimes destroyed. The greater the damage, the more likely a daughter is to have ongoing problems throughout her life: more anxiety and depression, lower self-confidence, lower rates of college and high school graduation, higher rates of teenage pregnancy and sexual diseases, more depression and eating disorders, and more troubled relationships with men.[2-17]

But not only do most daughters pay a price, so do most dads. When a divorced father doesn't get to spend enough time with his children, he is more depressed, anxious, and emotionally fragile.[18-21] He can also suffer for years from being "fired" as a parent by his children's doctors, teachers, and therapists.[22-24] And in his old age, a divorced father usually gets much less care and attention from his daughter than the mother gets.[25]

Sadly, divorce usually damages a daughter's relationship with her father more than a son's. Why? In part it's because a daughter is usually closer to her mom and the son closer to his dad before the divorce.[26] On top of that, too many divorced mothers lean too heavily on their daughters for advice and caretaking in ways that turn the daughter against her father.[27] Also, divorced dads tend to spend more time with their sons than with their daughters.[28] Daughters also tend to get more upset than sons by their parents' conflicts, which further complicates the father-daughter relationship.[29,30] Compared to sons, daughters are more likely to miss and to long for a relationship with their dads even years after their parents' divorce.[31-34]

If your relationship has been damaged by divorce, surely you have both wondered: "Why? Why did things fall apart for us? Who's to blame?" Daughters often place all—or almost all—of the blame on dad. Fathers often say they were pushed out of their daughter's life by a biased legal system, financial problems, and their ex-wives.

But why does it matter at this point where the blame lies? It matters because as long as a daughter blames most of the problems on her father, she may choose not to forgive him and choose not to give him a chance to rebuild their relationship. And it matters because if a father refuses to assume any of the responsibility, he won't be able to apologize or to talk candidly with his daughter about the issues that still separate them. As for who's right, neither—and both. Yes, most dads could have done more or could have behaved better after the divorce. *And so could most daughters and mothers.* So in that sense, all three share the blame. And, yes, there are barriers and forces working against divorced fathers, which is why the two of you need to talk honestly about what the barriers in your relationship were. But, yes again, there are fathers who essentially walk out on their daughters, regardless of how much encouragement they get to stay involved, though that is rare for fathers who have been married to their daughter's mother.

Because blame makes it harder to forgive and to rebuild, let's start by exploring the reasons why your relationship was damaged. By seeing that no one person and no one event was to blame, you can start to repair the damage—to rebuild and to reconnect.

Demoralizing and Demeaning Divorced Dads

If you're like most families, your time together after the divorce was restricted to four to six nights a month, a few hours one night each week, and a couple of weeks of vacation time. Roughly 85 to 90 percent of kids live with their mother after divorce; only 5 to 10 percent live at least one third of the time with their father. And half of all kids only see their father once or twice a year.[35-36] So as a daughter you still might be wondering: *Why didn't my dad spend more time with me? Did he lose interest in me?* And as a father, you might still be asking: *Why can't my daughter understand why I wasn't able to spend more time with her? When is she going to realize how heartbroken I was to be pushed out of her life?*

As we've discussed in an earlier chapter, we're surrounded by negative myths and half-truths about fathers. This is especially true when it comes to divorced fathers. For example, most television shows and movies encourage us to assume the worst about divorced dads. The typical divorced dad comes across as a childish, self-centered, irresponsible blockhead. Often he dumps his devoted wife and abandons his kids for a much younger woman—beautiful and dumb. While mom is struggling to make ends meet, dad is having the time of his life. Child support? Forget that. Dad's spending all his money on himself and his girlfriend. Fed up with the way movies demean divorced dads, director James Brooks made *Spanglish*, a movie where the father, for a change, is the far better parent to his daughter than the mother.[37] Is it any wonder that even well-educated college students describe divorced dads more negatively than gay dads, adoptive dads, and stepdads?[38]

As for your father-daughter relationship, remember: *The negative beliefs that you have about any group of people influence what you remember about how they behaved in the past and how you treat them—even when your beliefs are wrong.* This is why it's important to ask this question: What did you, as a daughter, believe about divorced dads at the time your parents divorced? By taking the "Divorced Dads: Bad Guys?" quiz on the next page, you can see which beliefs were affecting you then—and might still be affecting you now.

What's your score? Hopefully, zero. Not one of the statements is true, as you can see from the research in the "Divorced Dads: Facts Please" box. But the higher your score, the more likely it is that your negative beliefs about divorced fathers made it harder for your dad to maintain a good relationship

Divorced Dads: Bad Guys?

When your parents got divorced, what did you believe about divorced men?

True?

_____ Most divorces happen because the man falls in love with another woman.

_____ Most divorces happen because the husband is abusive, alcoholic, or unstable.

_____ Many divorces happen because the father committed adultery.

_____ Fathers generally lose interest in their children after a divorce.

_____ Financially most fathers are far better off than mothers after divorce.

_____ Mothers are usually more depressed than fathers after their divorce.

_____ College-educated mothers are rarely angry about money after divorce.

_____ The husband is usually the person who wants the divorce.

_____ Most divorced fathers do not make their child support payments.

_____ It is extremely rare for a mother to prevent the father from seeing the children.

_____ **Your score**   (10 True possible)

with you. You might have been duped years ago to believe these negative things about divorced dads. But you don't have to be duped now. You can open your eyes to the realities that divorced dads face. Then you can explore with your father what actually did happen at the time of his divorce.

Divorced Dads: Facts Please

- Most divorces are initiated by the wife because she doesn't feel her husband meets her emotional needs or communicates well enough—not because of adultery, physical abuse, or drug or alcohol problems.[39]
- Fathers are more likely than mothers to stay in an unhappy marriage for the sake of the kids.[40]
- More than 80 percent of divorced fathers pay their full child support.[41]
- Fathers are more depressed, stressed, and disheartened than mothers after divorce because they miss their children so much.[42]
- Most fathers are not much better off financially than mothers after divorce.[43, 44]
- Compared to less educated moms, college-educated, white mothers tend to be as angry or angrier about financial matters after divorce.[45–46]

As father and daughter, it's time to talk about how dad was treated as a parent after the divorce. Did he feel welcomed and valued as a father? How did your teachers, doctors, relatives, coaches, and neighbors treat him? Did these people dump your dad as a parent? Use "The Dumped Dad" quiz to talk about his

The Dumped Dad

How was your father treated after the divorce?

**? = not sure   0 = no/never   1 = rarely
2 = fairly often   3 = almost always/yes**

_____ My father was given almost equal time as our mom had with us kids.

_____ My relatives treated my father and mother equally as parents.

_____ My friends treated my dad the same way they did when my parents were married.

_____ My doctors, counselors, and teachers kept my father informed about me.

_____ My school sent information to my father just like they did to my mother.

_____ If I saw a therapist, he or she included my father in the counseling sessions.

_____ My teachers made sure my father was invited and welcomed in parent activities.

_____ My friends' parents continued to treat my father like a full-fledged parent.

_____ My dad was told far enough in advance about my activities so he could arrange to attend.

_____ Adults in our religious group continued to treat my father as a full-fledged parent.

_____ **Your score**   (30 possible)

[164]

experiences. You both have to agree on one thing: Neither of you is going to talk about your mother while you're doing this quiz. You are only going to talk about how the other adults treated your father.

As a father, you may have been luckier than most in terms of how the legal system treated you. Tell your daughter about your experiences with the people who were making the decisions about how much time you would be allowed to spend with her. As a daughter, you may already know how each of your parents felt about how much time you should spend with each of them. But if you haven't heard your father's side of the story, now's the time.

Tragically, there is still a strong bias against fathers in the legal system. Many lawyers and judges favor mothers in dividing the time between parents. Mediators, social workers, and psychologists tend to oppose letting fathers have anywhere near equal time with their children, especially if the children are young.[47-52] Yes, dads have the legal right to hire lawyers and fight for more time with the kids. But that takes lots of money and time. Not surprisingly, dads aren't a whole lot more likely than they were thirty years ago to get anywhere near equal time with their kids.[53] Obviously, we can't place all the blame on biased laws. There are fathers who choose not to spend time with their kids after divorce—men who weren't very involved with the kids during their marriage either. But the overwhelming majority of divorced dads wants and makes every effort to stay involved in their children's lives.

What Dads and Daughters Want—But Rarely Get
Given the barriers most dads are up against, it's not surprising that most fathers and daughters don't get what they both want—plenty of time together. As the Shared Parenting

research section below shows, dads and daughters want to spend—and ought to spend—much more time living together. Yet even years later, many are still sad or angry about how little time they got to spend together. Shared parenting means that the father and kids spend more than four to six days a month together, including enough time during the school week so dad can be actively involved in his child's everyday routines. Sadly, only 10 to 15 percent of fathers and daughters get to enjoy the benefits of shared parenting. Sadder still, more than a third of daughters and fathers only see each other a few times a year and only one third have weekly contact.[54]

Shared Parenting: Fact and Fiction

Fiction: Most children are satisfied with how much time they spend (or spent) with their fathers after their parents' divorce. As long as the mom has enough money, kids don't pay a price for too little fathering after divorce.

Fact: The vast majority of children say they want or wanted more time with their fathers. Those who don't get enough fathering after their parents' divorce are more likely to have social and psychological problems throughout their lives. [55-61]

Fiction: Divorced parents obviously can't get along well enough to share parenting so it's better that mom raise the kids.

Fact: Most parents can cooperate well enough to share parenting and most become more cooperative after attending parenting programs.[62-69]

Fiction: Infants and kids under five should live full-time with their mom because they are too young to spend nights at their dad's.

Fact: Infants and young children should not be away from either parent for more than a few days and are not disrupted by spending nights in both homes.[70–71]

Fiction: When kids spend more time living with dad, they will be worse off financially because their father will have to pay so much less child support.

Fact: The more time dad gets to spend with his kids, the more money he usually spends on child support and on voluntary expenses such as clothes, camps, and college educations.[72–73]

Fiction: Most divorced fathers don't want more parenting responsibility or more time with their kids.

Fact: The overwhelming majority of divorced fathers wants to spend more time with their kids and have more parenting responsibility.[74]

Fiction: Kids would rather live with mom than hassle with living in both parents' homes.

Fact: Kids who lived in both parents' homes on a regular basis preferred this to living with mom. Young adults who lived mainly with their mothers wish they had lived more with dad.[75]

Fiction: Fathers could have their kids live with them much more of the time if they really wanted to share the parenting.

Fact: Fathers often don't have enough money to set up a home suitable for kids to live in regularly or to hire lawyers to fight for shared parenting time. [76-77]

Money—The Never Ending Battle

The two issues that generally create the most tension between divorced fathers and daughters are the M and Ms: Money and Mothers. These two factors can make it very difficult—if not impossible—for many fathers and daughters to stay connected. So let's consider the first M—Money. How has money interfered with your relationship? And how can you repair the damage? Start by taking the "Money: From Both Points of View" quiz.

The higher your score, the more likely it is that you two had, or still have, some bad feelings having to do with money. Because most parents divorce when their children are young, it's easy for kids to become confused about what's going on financially. And with so many negative beliefs about divorced fathers floating around, it's easy for kids to assume the worst about their dad and money. Not all of the following facts will apply to your situation. But it's important to find out which ones do. By talking about these topics, you can clear the air about some of the misunderstandings that have damaged your relationship.

Like many, your relationship might have been damaged by the belief that fathers are much better off financially than mothers after divorce. This belief spread like wildfire twenty-five years ago after sociologist Lenore Weitzman wrote a book claiming that a woman's standard of living fell by 73 percent and a man's rose by 42 percent after divorce. [78] There's only one problem—Weitzman was wrong! It took ten years for her to admit her mistake—and only after many researchers had

Money: From Both Points of View

Dad: How often did you feel that your daughter thought these things about you?

Daughter: Did you feel that your father was like this?

Dad: 0 = never 1 = rarely 2 = usually 3 = almost always

Daughter: 0 = no 1 = maybe 2 = probably 3 = definitely

Dad   Daughter

_____ _____ Dad is stingy and greedy.

_____ _____ Dad didn't treat my mom fairly in terms of money.

_____ _____ Dad shouldn't complain about how mom spends his child support money.

_____ _____ Dad should pay for college since he makes more money than mom.

_____ _____ Mom shouldn't have to spend the same percentage of her income on us kids as dad.

_____ _____ If it weren't for dad, mom would be better off financially.

_____ _____ It's not fair that dad is better off financially than mom.

_____ _____ If it weren't for mom, dad wouldn't be the success he is financially.

_____ _____ My father didn't pay—or isn't paying—all of his child support.

_____ _____ Dad didn't make financial sacrifices like mom did after the divorce.

_____ _____ **Your scores** (30 possible)

[169]

studied her data and protested that she had done a great injustice to divorced men. In her small study of high-income couples, by the second year after divorce, many of the women had remarried and had the same incomes as before the divorce. The study also didn't count the house as part of the woman's wealth, making it look as if she was much poorer than she actually was.[79]

Hopefully as a daughter, when your parents divorced, you realized that most men do not end up far better off than women. On top of child support, most fathers are paying for the children's health insurance, additional clothing, toys, camps, recreational expenses, and college educations. In the largest federally funded study ever conducted, fathers were left with only $25 a month more than mothers. In short, most divorced dads are struggling financially just as much as their ex-wives.[80]

As a father, let's hope your daughter has always understood that her mom got half of everything; the house, car, savings, and retirement accounts. If she believes you shortchanged her mother, that's bound to create some ill feelings toward you. So take time to explain what happened financially. It's time to set the record straight. If you did shortchange her mother, or failed to pay all your child support, or didn't help pay for college—why not? If you owe your daughter an apology, do so, the sooner the better. If you can make amends by helping her out now financially, do it!

Especially during the college years, money can damage your relationship. You may be facing (or have already faced) tough issues like these: How much should a father pay if his daughter has refused to have much contact with him? If dad is chipping in, how much say should he have in what college she chooses? What if he is willing to pay for a state university but not for an expensive private school? What if mom refuses to pay anything because dad makes more money than she does? What if mom claims she can't afford to help out, but dad says she can—so he refuses to pay unless she pays? If any of these issues is still bothering either of you, it's time to talk them through.

Finally, money is troublesome when a dad feels that his daughter cares as much about his money as she does about him. As the old saying goes, "When his money stops coming through the door, her love flies out the window." If you feel this way, dad, tell your daughter what she did, or is still doing, that makes you feel she is measuring your love by how much money you give her. Let her know how much this hurts. Then make a plan that will put a stop to this pain.

Mother: Dad's Ally?

The M and Ms—Money and Mothers. Mothers have a tremendous impact on the father-daughter relationship, as we discussed in an earlier chapter. But after a divorce, mom enjoys a major power surge. Zap! Boom! Since most kids live with mom, dad's power shrinks while mom's expands. Many moms are to be congratulated for using this power to keep the kids closely bonded to their dads. Unfortunately, too many moms have a hard time using their power in this positive way. Although a mom may never come right out and say bad things about dad, she can undermine him in other ways—the expressions on her face, her tone of voice, the way she treats dad when he comes to pick up the kids, the way she acts before the kids leave to be with him. So ask yourself which message got through to you: *"Your dad's a jerk who broke up our family and he's never been as good a parent as I am,"* or *"Both your dad and I made mistakes that led to our divorce; but we're both good parents."*

As the research in the "Divorced Mother" section below shows, too many moms don't cooperate with dad. Some don't want him to be an equal parent in any sense of the word. Others unknowingly do damage by sharing information about the marriage and divorce that weakens the father-child bond. By allowing or encouraging the kids to feel sorry for her, a mom can sometimes bind them to her in ways that hurt their relationship with their dad, as you can see from the "Miserable Mom, Happy Dad?" quiz. Hopefully in your family, the kids didn't feel sorrier for mom than for dad—and didn't see mom as the weak, frail person, while dad was the powerful, strong one.

The higher the scores, the more likely it is that their relationship made it through the divorce in pretty good shape. For the sake of the father-daughter relationship, we want the daughter to feel that both parents are building joyful lives for themselves, so she won't feel disloyal or guilty about being close to dad. The daughter shouldn't become her mother's emotional service station—the place where mom goes for a refill of comfort, advice, guidance, self-confidence, or general pumping up. But the bottom line is this: If dad feels that his ex-wife is shutting him out of the children's lives or turning the kids against him, he may gradually lose hope and become so disheartened that he backs away as the years pass.

Divorced Mother: Dad's Ally?

- Mothers tend to stay angrier longer and refuse to forgive more than fathers after divorce.[81]

- Many programs for divorced parents are aimed at convincing moms to allow dads to be involved in their children's lives.[82, 83]

Miserable Mom, Happy Dad?

How do you think your parents were after their divorce? Read the following statements and rank each of them based on the scale.

0 = never   1 = rarely
2 = quite a bit   3 = almost always

Mom   Dad

_____ _____ I am relatively happy.

_____ _____ I am taking care of myself emotionally and financially without help from my kids.

_____ _____ I don't need or want my kids to worry about me.

_____ _____ I don't need or want my kids to feel sorry for me.

_____ _____ In time, I will be as happy as I was before the divorce.

_____ _____ My adult friends can help me solve my problems.

_____ _____ I was upset by the divorce, but I'm recovering more and more as time passes.

_____ _____ I get pleasure from doing activities other than with the kids.

_____ _____ I hope someday to get married again.

_____ _____ Feels optimistic about the future.

_____ _____ **Your scores** (30 possible)

[173]

- Many divorced mothers admit that they have denied visitation or made it extremely difficult for the father to see the children, and they don't want to share the parenting.[84–88]

- Many young adults say that when it came to criticizing, badmouthing, and demeaning the other parent, their mothers were worse than their fathers after the divorce.[89, 90]

- Roughly one third of mothers move the kids four to five hundred miles away from their fathers within the first two years of divorce, drastically reducing the time that fathers and children spend together.[91]

Divorced Dads: Dumped & Demoralized

What advice would you give these dads? What have their daughters failed to understand?

"My daughter always wants me to drive into the city to take her to dinner or to take her shopping. She also expects me to keep paying her rent until she saves up more money. But there's never any compromise on her part. She only lives thirty minutes away. But she never comes to my home and refuses to call my house because she doesn't want to talk to my fiancée. She's refusing to come to my wedding next May. Should I lay down the law and insist that my daughter respect my new life and spend time with me and my fiancée? Should I refuse to keep supporting her unless she agrees to come to my wedding?"

"My daughter lived with me for five years because she and her mom didn't get along. But when she turned sixteen, she said she wanted to go live with her mother—just see me every other weekend. I was in shock. Of course, I didn't force her to keep living with me. But she seems to grow more and more distant. Sometimes she's actually hateful towards me. When I ask what's wrong, she says Nothing. Is there a point where I should stop seeing her until she starts treating me better?"

"My twenty-four-year-old daughter is extremely jealous of my wife and stepdaughter. Her favorite saying is 'My unhappiness is all your fault!' For years I have been receiving counseling, reading self-help books, and changing the way I communicate with her to show her my love. But nothing seems to be good enough. Now she's mad at me because yesterday I didn't hear my cell phone ringing when she called. She accused me of not answering because I was with my wife and stepdaughter. When I tell her that I need her love just like she needs mine, she says I can get all the love I need from my wife and stepdaughter. I feel that my "little princess" has become manipulative and self-centered. This has been going on for more than a year. Is there still hope? Should I give up?"

African American Dads: Baby's Mama Drama

Like white daughters, too many black daughters whose parents don't live together get the message from mom that dad isn't all that necessary.[92] Especially if dad isn't pitching in any money, mom may be teaching her daughter that women can get along just fine without husbands or fathers. And if mom feels this way, dad and daughter usually drift apart.

Many black dads feel that they are driven away by "baby's mama drama"—a situation where the dad feels that all the mom wants is his money. From dad's point of view, mom's goal is to make him as miserable as possible by creating dramas that cause him to back away from their kids.[93] As the singer Hollister puts it:

"I gots the baby mama drama.
Enough to wanna make ya scream and holla.
She trying to get me for my dollas.
Aint nuthin' but that baby mama drama."[94]

Here's how several black fathers explain it:

> *"Most of the brothers I grew up with did so without a father. This adversely affected our thought patterns, attitudes, values, and beliefs. For example, most men I know sincerely believe that as long as they go to work and pay the bills, there is an unwritten right for us to pretty much do as we please."*

> *"Nothing that I do ever seems to be enough for the mother of my little girl. While I love my children, I wish I had never met their mother."*

> *"Every weekend it is something else with her. The drama never ends! She seems bent on making my life hell because things did not work out between us. All I want to do is be there for my children."*[95]

This isn't to say that most black mothers create mama-drama, or that the drama is mainly the woman's fault.

Clearly there are African American moms who encourage and allow the dad to be involved in the children's lives, even when he isn't contributing any money.[96] Still, like the white mother, the black mother holds the key to the gate between dad and the kids. And when mom isn't happy with dad, she usually locks the gate—especially if she has a new man in her life.[97-99]

Dad Remarries: Oh Happy Days!

Things generally get tougher when "that woman" becomes dad's wife. As a daughter, maybe you felt that dad picked the wrong woman or remarried too soon. Maybe you felt he loved her—or their child—more than he loved you. As a father, maybe you felt that your daughter was (or still is) being unfair and unkind to you and your wife. What's going on? Why is dad's remarriage creating bad feelings?

Well, here come the M and Ms again: Mom and Money. Both play a major hand in how everyone reacts to dad's new marriage. If mom is happy about it—or if she's completely indifferent—then things generally go much better for dad, daughter, and dad's wife. But, as the old saying goes, "If mama ain't happy, ain't *nobody* happy!" Unfortunately, many mothers are not happy when dad remarries. Looking back, these daughters sum it up these ways:

> "Mom was always telling us that dad was nicer to her and to us kids before he remarried. So I resented him and his wife. Now I realize that mom was just mad because he had fallen in love and things fell apart between her and the man she left dad for."

[177]

"Dad and his wife had successful careers and really good incomes. So mom would say, 'I'm not a materialistic person who needs a lot of money.' This was her way of criticizing my dad and his wife, trying to make them look like materialistic, greedy people. I fell for it."

"Yeah, mom would tell me to have a good time whenever I went to see my dad and his wife. But she'd look really sad and tell me how much she was going to miss me. I'd feel sorry for her. So I'd call her and try to make her feel better by saying that I wasn't having a very good time. Even now when I go home to visit my parents, I go to her place first so that she won't feel jealous."

"Mom exploded when the school listed my stepmother as one of the people to contact in case of emergencies. Things like that made me feel that my stepmom had no right to be part of my life."

Money also comes into play. Especially if dad has a child with his new wife, his daughter might start wondering: "How much of his money is he spending on them instead of on me? Why is he buying his wife so much stuff when he says he can't afford to buy certain things for me or for my kids? When dad dies, are his wife or her kids going to end up with the family heirlooms or with more money than me or my kids?" If you haven't gotten these things out in the open, it's time. And the sooner, the better. Let's be honest: When people say "it's not the money, it's the principle of the thing," it usually *is* the money! Remember too, people can get really upset about who gets what after dad dies, even when the things aren't worth much. That old, chipped platter that was used every Thanksgiving might only be worth $5, but heaven help us if dad's wife gets it after he dies!

Daughters in Distress: Dad's Marriage

What advice would you give to these daughters? What have these dads and daughters failed to understand?

"I am a thirty-five-year-old married mom with a five-year-old daughter. My parents divorced when I was thirteen. My mom was mentally ill, so I lived with my dad. He was Super Man and the most important person in my life. The major breakdown in my relationship with him started when I was in my early twenties and he started dating a woman who is fifteen years younger than he is. Even since they got married, my image of my father has crumbled because he has made her his number-one priority. He is always focused and doting on her. He seems terrified of losing her. After years of tension over this, yesterday he called and said that he was fed up with the way I have treated her. I told him I felt unloved because he treats her better than he treats me and my daughter. I told him that no matter how old my daughter gets to be, she will always be my baby. And I told him I was mad that he didn't make the trip cross country to visit me more often. I'm the one who has to do most of the traveling to see him. He hung up on me. Do you think at this point I should let this relationship, which is hanging by a thread, go ahead and die?"

"My mom died when I was a teenager. Fortunately, my dad and I had a wonderful relationship. But now it seems to be changing. He's going to marry the woman he has been dating for a couple of years. I'm thirty-four now. And here is the dream I had last night: My mom, dad, and I are in the living room of our old house on Birch Street. Mom says to dad, 'Well, I'm back, just like you always wanted.' He says 'Oh, wow. This isn't what I expected. I'm getting remarried. Can I have time to think about this?' Mom didn't answer him, but I did, 'If you choose that other woman over my mother, then I choose my mother over you!' When I woke up this morning, I was so mad at my dad. What's this all about?"

"My parents divorced when I was six. I lived in the Midwest with mom when dad moved to Florida, remarried, and had five more kids. I did shuttle diplomacy for years to visit him. He was a workaholic who never seemed to have much time for me. Now that he's seventy and retired, I've been asking him to come visit. But he always makes an excuse about not being well enough. I'm unwilling to visit him because he's got more spare time than I do. Suggestions?"

Along with money and mothers, another barrier often arises when dad remarries—jealousy, his daughter's and his wife's. Many daughters don't realize that a father's love is not like a pie with a limited number of pieces to be handed out— one piece for each of his other children, one piece for his new wife, and then oops! No piece left for you. Your father has enough love for everyone, but his wife and daughter might be jealously competing for it.

The solution? Dad's wife, encourage your husband to spend lots of time with his daughter without you around. Dad, use the time to focus on your daughter, not to talk about your new wife or her kids. Daughter, if you feel jealous or left out, tell your dad how you feel and ask him to spend more time with you. And when you ask, don't make mean-spirited or snide remarks about his wife or other kids. Try saying something like this: "Dad, I know this might sound silly, but I'm feeling a little jealous and left out. I'd really like to have more time alone with you. Could we meet for dinner or lunch next week? Could we set aside one afternoon a month to hang out together?"

As a daughter, have you ever felt that your father is a better parent to his new kids than he was to you? If you're right, hurrah for him! I hope he *is* a better father now than he was in the past. That means he's a sensitive, well-meaning guy. He's trying to be a better father and that's admirable. If he was still making the same mistakes you think he made with you, why would that make you happy? What's really bothering you? Are you angry or jealous because you wish he had given you what he's giving them? Well, here's the good news: You can have your share of the new, improved dad. What's stopping you from reaching out for what he now has to offer you? If he's less focused on work and more focused on family nowadays, then spend more time with him. If he's not as tense as he was as a young father, good for you—enjoy it. Stop blaming him for becoming a better father. *Embrace the father he has become.*

As a dad, my bet is you have already made the mistake of trying to convince your daughter to become friends with your new wife. Understandable—but a big mistake. We're bombarded with the message that "step" families are supposed to blend well. Even when the daughter never lived with her dad and his wife while she was growing up, everyone can feel that the two women are supposed to bond. Worse yet, we assume that if a daughter loves her dad, she will accept his new wife with open arms. Accepting his wife becomes a test of the daughter's love. And when this doesn't happen, everyone feels miserable. Dad is hurt. His daughter is angry. And his wife is disheartened because no matter how hard she tries, she's still the evil stepmother.

What to do? First, stop trying to live up to the blended family fairy tales. This will take the pressure off everyone. Start with these more realistic, relaxing assumptions: Dads and daughters should never have to "approve of" or become friends with the other's spouse. We've already talked about the difference between approving and accepting. Yes, you need to accept your dad's wife. And, yes, he needs to accept your husband or boyfriend. If you and his wife or he and your husband/boyfriend eventually become friends, that's fine. But it's not essential and not a test of how much father and daughter love each other. *What is* essential is that everyone be cordial and that nobody pressures anybody into anything beyond cordiality.

So is it all right for a daughter to refuse to go to her dad's wedding, refuse to celebrate a holiday with him and his wife, or refuse to call their home because she doesn't want to have to talk to the wife if she answers? Should a daughter allow "that woman" to be a grandmother to her kids? Answer these questions yourself by reversing the situation: If a father doesn't like his daughter's fiancé, is it all right for him to refuse to go to her wedding, refuse to call their home, refuse to celebrate a holiday with them, and refuse to be a grandfather to their kids? Whatever decisions you make, remember that the "rules" are the same for both sides. So choose carefully.

Are You an Evil Stepdaughter?

Are you friendly to your father's wife? How often have you done these things?

0 = never   1 = rarely   2 = fairly often   3 = almost always

_____ Thanked her for something she's done for your dad.

_____ Told her you appreciate how happy she makes your dad.

_____ Shown any interest in her childhood, family, and friends.

_____ Asked any questions about what's going on in her life.

_____ Wished her a happy birthday.

_____ Complimented her for anything.

_____ Said something nice about her child or her relatives.

_____ Included her in the pictures you take of the family.

_____ Used a friendly voice when you've asked to speak to your dad on the phone.

_____ Thanked her for nice things she has done for you or your family.

_____ **Your score** (30 possible)

Let's assume the worst: Years have passed, but no matter how hard everyone has tried, daughter and dad's wife are miserable being around each other, even for short periods of time. And that makes dad miserable too. In that case, let it go. There's no sense putting such a strain on dad's relationship with his daughter or his wife. It's not the end of the world. Dad and his daughter can continue to have good times together. Just remember: Dad, don't pressure your daughter to give your wife another chance. Don't spend the time talking about how great your wife is. Daughter, don't make any negative or snide remarks about his wife. Dad's wife, don't keep reminding your husband how hurt you are by the way his daughter treats you. Focus on your marriage, not on your relationship with his daughter.

Our "Evil" Stepmothers

As a daughter or father, what advice would you give these wives?

"I am heartbroken by the rift between my husband and his daughter. It's been nearly a year since she refused contact with us. Her parents' angry divorce when she was a teenager and her own difficult marriage are big factors in this current rift. But the two grandkids have become the pawns. We have been cut out of their lives. We have tried calling and sending letters, emails, and cards. No response. Even the grandkids' birthday presents were returned unopened, marked 'Return to Sender.' Can we do anything other than wait for her to decide she wants us back in her life?"

"My husband and his ex-wife shared custody of their daughter until he met me. His daughter is hurt and upset because we had a child. When he called to tell her that she had a healthy baby brother, her mother snatched the phone away and told my husband never to call again if it had to do with "that baby." He suggested that he and his daughter go to counseling. But she refused to agree to it. His daughter refuses to mend her relationship with her loving, patient father. What can we do?"

"My teenage stepdaughter has decided she doesn't want to see her dad anymore. But she won't tell him why. We feel helpless and blocked at every turn. We don't even know what happened since neither the mother or his daughter's therapist will tell us anything about what's going on. Where do we go from here?"

"My husband is a warm and loving, well-educated and successful attorney—in other words, no slacker. But his thirty-year-old daughter doesn't want much to do with him. His ex-wife had a terrible relationship with her father. And even though she left my husband for another man, she makes his daughter feel that having a relationship with him is being disloyal to her. Is there any way things can change unless the mother releases her from this emotional bondage? In the meantime, my husband suffers. How can I help?"

The Blame Game: Lousy Husband, Lousy Father?

Many relationships are strained—or have ended—because the daughter continues to blame her father for the divorce. She figures that if dad was a lousy husband, he should lose the right to be her father. As Gabby says, "If it hadn't been for dad, they would still be married and my mom and I wouldn't have had to go through hell. Why should I give him a second chance given how he betrayed mom? If I forgive him, I would be saying what he did wasn't wrong. It would be disloyal to mom for me to overlook what he did."

It might seem okay to punish dad for his "sins" as a husband. But daughters who do this are sticking their nose into their parents' business—and taking on a dangerous role as judge and prosecutor. Let's reconsider Gabby's choices. First, if

[185]

Gabby knows for certain that her father cheated, why is she assuming that his infidelity is the *only* reason—or the main reason—that the marriage ended? Isn't it highly likely there were longstanding problems in the marriage, problems having to do with Gabby's mother, or money, or meddling in-laws, or...? Second, if Gabby accepts the fact that both parents were probably responsible for their eroding marriage, this doesn't mean she has to excuse or to overlook her dad's infidelity. Cheating is wrong—period. But Gabby doesn't have to *choose* to punish her father for his shortcomings as a husband.

Third, Gabby is old enough to face reality: A person can be a lousy spouse and still be a good parent. For example, just because someone commits adultery, is emotionally abusive or is cold and withdrawn with their spouse, doesn't automatically mean that he or she can't be a good mother or father. Yes, some people are terrible spouses and terrible parents. But more often than not, daughters are punishing their fathers for being grade "D" husbands even when they are "A," "B," or "C" fathers. That's unfair, unloving, and unwise. If you as a daughter think your dad was a failure as a husband, then don't marry a man like him. But if he was getting a passing grade as a father before the divorce, then why are you flunking him now? Why do that to yourself? Why do that to him?

Finally, Gabby is punishing her father because she's only considering the mistakes he made—not mistakes that she probably made—after her parents divorced. If her father is willing to forgive her for the mean or insensitive things that she did to him, then why can't she do the same? As a father and a daughter, surely each of you can admit that there are things you could have done better—things you wish you had done differently. Use the questions in the "Our Mistakes" box to jump-start your conversation—and to apologize and forgive.

Our Mistakes

What three things have you each done since the divorce that have hurt your relationship?

Daughter _____

Dad _____

What do you wish each of you had done instead?

Daughter _____

Dad _____

What are three things you did that were good for your relationship after the divorce?

Daughter _____

Dad _____

Reconnecting: Starting Over

Nothing is more heartbreaking than daughters and fathers who haven't seen each other for years as a result of things that happened after the parents' divorce. These daughters and fathers tell me that they are afraid to contact one another for three reasons. First, they both believe that the other person no longer loves them. Second, the father believes that his daughter will never forgive him because of mistakes he made. Third, they don't know how to take the first step to get back together.

The irony is that, regardless of how much time has passed since they've spoken, fathers and daughters rarely stop loving—or wondering about—one another. The longing may have become a silent, deep ache that only surfaces when they are reminded of one another—seeing a little girl who looks a lot like the daughter did as a child, seeing another daughter walking hand-in-hand with her elderly father, hearing a song that dad used to sing to his daughter, watching a movie where dad is walking his daughter down the aisle. The ache is still there. The longing and the wondering: *What's her life like? What's become of him? Am I forgotten? If one of us was dying, would that bring us back together?*

Sadly, while fathers and daughters continue to long for a relationship, neither reaches out. Why? It is usually because they're afraid. Afraid of what? Mainly, they are afraid of being rejected. But there are other fears holding them back as well. So the first step is to figure out exactly what you're afraid of. Use the box on page 190 to identify your fears and to imagine how you would feel if the worst happened. Would you feel sadder, more abandoned, or lonelier than you do now? I doubt it. What have you got to lose? Now think about what you stand to gain.

As for the father's fear that his daughter won't forgive him, yes, that's possible. Your daughter might not be ready yet to let you back into her life. But that's highly unlikely. And even if she isn't ready now, you can open the door for her to come back to you later. In twenty years of working with young adult daughters, I can tell you that *not one* has ever refused to let her father back into her life (except three daughters whose fathers had physically or sexually abused them).

Treating Dad Like a Second-Class Parent

Since the divorce, how have you treated your father?

0 = never 1 = rarely 2 = usually 3 = almost always

_____ I spend more time visiting my mother than my dad.

_____ I spend more holidays with mom than with dad.

_____ I put more thought into the gifts I give my mother than those I give him.

_____ I phone my mother more often than I phone him.

_____ I do more to celebrate mom's birthday or Mother's Day than dad's birthday or Father's Day.

_____ I plan my visits first with mom, then let dad know when I'm free to see him.

_____ I spend the most important part of the holidays with mom.

_____ I invite my friends to mom's house more often than to dad's house.

_____ I spend as much time with dad's relatives as with mom's relatives.

_____ I talk more with mom than with dad about their marriage and divorce.

_____ **Your score** (30 possible)

What Are You Afraid Of?

*What are you afraid would happen if you contacted
each other? How likely are those things to happen? How
would you feel if they did happen?*

My Fears	How likely is it to happen?	How painful would it be?
would refuse to see me	_____	
wouldn't forgive me	_____	
mother would get upset	_____	
would hang up on me	_____	
wouldn't answer my letter	_____	
would get mad at me	_____	
would bring up things I don't want to talk about	_____	
wouldn't know what to say	_____	
one of us might cry	_____	

Now make a list of the good things that might happen.

_____

_____

_____

All of their fathers did what you, as a father, must do, which is:

1) Contact your daughter instead of waiting for her to contact you.

2) Apologize for the things you did that contributed to the rift between you. Be specific about your mistakes and tell her what you wish you had done differently.

3) Don't blame or say anything negative about her mother.

4) Reassure her that you're not expecting her to treat you as if nothing had happened or to automatically accept you as a full-fledged dad. Tell her that rebuilding your relationship will take time— and that you're 100 percent committed to putting time into it.

5) Let her know that you understand her fear of being abandoned—and her fear of being disappointed and heartbroken again. Because your daughter probably feels that you abandoned her, she's afraid to trust you. That makes sense. After all, she's afraid you might walk out on her again. Tell her that your verbal promises aren't going to be enough. Tell her that it's the way you treat her from here on that's going to build her trust.

6) Finally, put the power in her hands. If she feels that you dumped her, she has felt powerless—powerless to bring you back into her life, powerless to make you love her. Give her the power to tell you what she wants from you and to tell you how she wants you to relate to her. In the beginning, as you start to rebuild, let her be in control of the speed and the direction of your relationship. For example, you can say to her: "You tell me how often you want us to get together or talk on the phone. You tell me when it's okay for me to meet your kids and your husband. You let me know what you do or don't want to talk about as we're getting to know each other again." As your relationship develops, you can have more input into what you need and want. But in the beginning, let your daughter have most of the power. It helps build trust.

What to Say?

The next step is figuring out what to say. After all this time, how do you start? If you're too afraid to call, then start with a letter or an email. A sample letter is below. No matter how you word your letter, follow these guidelines:

1) *Make it clear that all you want is to renew your relationship.*
2) *Explain why you've been afraid to get in touch before now.*
3) *Promise that you're not going to bring her mother or other siblings into this.*
4) *Offer at least one specific suggestion for how the two of you might start to rebuild.*
5) *Don't bring up any big issues.*
6) *If you feel like apologizing for anything you've done, go right ahead.*
7) *Include a recent picture of yourself with the letter.*

The Letter—What to Say?

It's taken me a long time to get up the nerve to write you. I've been afraid that you wouldn't answer or that you'll send me an angry response. I don't know exactly how to start or what to say, except that I want us to be in touch again. Nobody has put me up to writing to you. And I don't want anyone else in the family to get involved in our relationship from here on.

There's nothing I need from you—other than to have you back in my life. I understand things about what happened between us a lot better now. And I have some things I want to apologize for. Could we have a phone call and see how that goes? Enclosed is a picture of me from a few months ago. Would you send me one of you? Well, I guess that's about it for now.

Is It Worth It?

When you take steps to undo the damage done by the divorce, will it be worth it? Let me start by sharing this note from a dad whose daughter, after two years of refusing his offers to get together, finally changed her mind: "On Thursday, October 10, I was awakened from a deep sleep with a phone call at 5 a.m. It sounded like my daughter. At first I thought someone was playing a cruel trick on me. But after she told me her middle name and the name of her cat, I knew it was her. I started crying like a baby. We talked for an hour. And we made plans to meet. This is our beginning. She told me she was tired of being angry."

Let me also share what daughters have to say after allowing their dads to talk about the divorce and after taking the step to contact their dads after many years:

> **Rita:** *"As we talked, he actually admitted that he should have worked harder at his marriage to my mother. With regret in his voice, he said the saddest part of his life was not being around us kids enough after the divorce. And he said he wished he had been more personal and loving in communicating with me. I never imagined he would apologize."*

Jody: *"Problems in my family are never discussed or explained—just ignored. Now, ten years after my parents' divorce, because of this talk with my dad, I learned all the missing pieces leading up to the breakup. I left him feeling I'd finally found someone who loves me and who had been taken away from me."*

Michelle: *"One of my father's comments cut straight to my heart. When we were discussing his dreams, he said he wonders if he will ever marry again. The expressive look on his face and tone of his voice showed me how much the divorce had hurt him. I stopped feeling mad at him because I saw him as a man with a lonely heart."*

Mary: *"Hearing my father's story made me uncomfortable because I've tried so hard to maintain a positive image of my mother. After much thought, I decided that it's still possible for me to admire her even though I see that what he told me about the way she treated him in their marriage and after the divorce is true."*

Roseanne: *"After letting him talk, I realize that he had to give up half his wealth when they divorced. Especially since my mom remarried so soon, he feels that his money is being used for her to enjoy life with another man. Finally I see his side, not just hers."*

Lynette: *"It had been five years since I'd seen my dad. I never thought I would get any response. But when I sent him the letter, he immediately emailed back. He actually called himself a failure regarding my sister and me. I realize that by taking my stepfather's last name, I made my* *dad feel I didn't love him. He said my contacting him was the best gift I had ever given him. I realize that seeing mom constantly upset by him while I was growing up had a profound effect on the way I felt about him. Now I want to focus on my issues with him—not on hers."*

Alex: *"The picture he said was most meaningful to him was just the two of us together when I was a little girl. When I asked him if I could have the picture to take back home with me, he wouldn't let me because for all these years he has kept it hanging in his bedroom. That made me cry. As I drove back to my place, I had a feeling I've never had after spending time with him: I felt that I was leaving home rather than coming home."*

Sex: Let's Stop Pretending   8

❖

- *I don't like the guy my daughter is dating. What should I do?*
- *My dad thinks I'm too young to get married. So I haven't told him that I'm engaged.*
- *Even at my age I lie to my dad about my private life. What's wrong with that?*
- *Why doesn't my daughter ever tell me anything about her relationships? It hurts my feelings.*
- *I don't know how to tell my dad that my female friend is more than a friend.*
- *Why does my daughter treat me like such an uptight guy?*
- *My father wouldn't respect me if he knew who I really am. So I pretend to be the innocent virgin.*
- *My daughter is in a terrible marriage. I'd like to talk to her about it. Should I?*
- *My father won't accept my husband because of his race. How can I get my father to see what a racist he is?*
- *My daughter wants me to act and dress like an old man. What's up with her?*

If you two are like most daughters and fathers, issues having to do with the daughter's sexual or romantic life have sometimes put a strain on your relationship. In most American families the teenage scene goes like this: When a daughter's "little girl" body begins turning into the "young woman" body, one of the parents has to have "the talk." Almost always it's mom and almost always mom talks about only two things: the details of menstruating and warnings about not getting pregnant. Rarely is dad involved in "the talk." From that point on, daughter and dad are usually too uncomfortable to talk about anything related to her body—her cramps or menstrual migraines, tampons, bras, underarm hair, bikini waxes, deodorant, or any medical problems of a "female" nature.

As for dating, dad's advice is usually limited to warnings: "Don't get pregnant. Boys are only after one thing. Boys don't marry girls with bad reputations." Once she graduates from high school until she marries, daughter and dad usually adopt the "don't ask, don't tell" policy. He doesn't ask anything about her "personal or private" life or about her "lifestyle"—code words for "sex," right? And she doesn't tell, even when that means lying repeatedly to her father.

Unfortunately, dealing with the daughter's sexuality in this way has a negative impact on her relationship with her father—an impact that usually lasts the rest of her life. How so? First, the daughter loses a lifelong advisor and ally on matters of the heart—her father. Having learned early in her life that sex, dating, and female body "stuff" are things girls should never discuss with their fathers, the adult daughter isn't likely to turn to her father for advice or for comfort on some of the most important parts of her life: decisions about marriage, troubles with boyfriends or with her husband, rape, unwanted pregnancies, a physically abusive relationship, or "female" health problems. The teenage girl who never talks to her dad about boyfriends, her menstrual migraine headaches, or her weight problem often ends up being the forty-year-old daughter who can't talk to her father about her crumbling marriage, the frightening results of her mammogram, or the boyfriend who hit her. And that's a tremendous loss—not just for the daughter, but for her father as well.

So first, let's figure out how you, as father and daughter, got to the place where you are now in dealing with the daughter's love life. Then let's consider ways to make your father-daughter relationship more relaxed when it comes to your private lives.

Speaking of Sex

- Teenage daughters whose fathers talk to them about sex and dating are less likely to have sex at an early age, get pregnant, or catch a sexual disease.[1,2]
- Daughters from father-absent homes are the most likely to get pregnant, contract sexual diseases, and have sex at an early age.[3,4]
- The Dutch believe that young people can be in love and that it's important to be in love before having sex. In the United States, most parents believe teenagers are too young to really fall in love.[5]
- Teenagers in the United States are more likely to get pregnant, catch a sexual disease, and have sex at a younger age than teens in other industrialized countries.[6]
- Teenagers from very religious families are just as likely to have premarital sex as children from less religious families.[7]
- Fathers are usually more unhappy about *who* their college-aged daughter chooses to have sex with than

about the fact that she is having sex.[8]

• Teenage pregnancies have fallen 10 percent since 2000 and 35 percent since 1990.[9]

Checkups: What Do You Believe?

Do you each know what the other *currently* believes about sex and controversial social issues? Before you say yes, think carefully. When is the last time you had a serious talk—just the two of you in private so that nobody else could judge or interfere—about any of these topics: premarital sex, abortion, how to decide when it's the right time or who the right person is to marry, drug use, drinking, gay or lesbian relationships, out-of-wedlock children? Are you both assuming that the way you felt and behaved ten years ago—or even five years ago—is the way you feel and would behave now? Daughters, are you assuming that because your dad was upset when he found out what you and your boyfriend were doing in high school, he's going to react the same way now if he finds out you're living with your boyfriend? Are you assuming that because he didn't want you to drink or to wear "that kind" of bikini when you were fifteen, he wants you to be a thirty-year-old virgin wearing a one-piece bathing suit and refusing a glass of wine? Dads, are you assuming that because your daughter had such goofy ideas about sex, drugs, or drinking in her younger years, she hasn't matured and changed? If so, it's time for a checkup on what both of you currently believe.

The important word here is *assuming*. Yes, some fathers do have the same conservative views they had when their daughters were teenagers. I'm sure you can find a father who wants his thirty-year-old daughter to be a virgin in a one-piece bathing suit who has never had a drink in her life. And, yes, there are daughters who are still behaving in the same goofy, self-destructive ways they did as teenagers when it comes to sex, dating, and drinking. But fathers and daughters shouldn't assume things about each other until they have updated their assumptions.

Generally speaking, most daughters make the mistake of assuming that dad is much more conservative and uptight than he actually is. And most fathers make the mistake of assuming that daughter is much more liberal than she actually is. For the sake of your *current* father-daughter relationship, don't assume you know what the other person believes about controversial issues such as premarital sex, abortion, gay and lesbian relationships, or drug or alcohol use. Get a checkup. Be sure your information and assumptions are current. Start your checkup by taking the "Dad's Uptight Generation?" quiz

 QUIZ

Dad's Uptight Generation?

What do you believe about most fathers who are now between the ages of forty-five and sixty-five? Answer true or false.

_____ Most were virgins when they got married.

_____ Most have only been married once.

_____ Most didn't have sex until they were in their twenties.

_____ Most married a woman who was a virgin.

_____ Most disapprove of their adult children having sex before marriage.

_____ Most never drank or smoked cigarettes as teenagers.

_____ Most have never used an illegal drug.

_____ Most are against sex education in the schools.

_____ Most want the laws changed so that abortion becomes illegal again.

_____ Most believe interracial marriages should be outlawed again.

and answering the questions in the "Your Experiences and Beliefs" section and talking about your answers together.

How many did you think were true? Hopefully, none. Not one of these statements is true about the majority of fathers.[10–12] Among adults who are now younger than seventy, only 10 percent of the men and 15 percent of the women were virgins when they married. Nearly 80 percent had sex, drank, smoked, and used recreational drugs as teenagers. More than half have been divorced at least once. Nearly a third of the women were pregnant before their wedding. Interracial and interfaith marriages increased dramatically during the 1960s and 1970s. And laws were changed so that today's generation has the legal right to terminate an unwanted pregnancy, to marry someone of another race, not to be fired for being gay, and not to be arrested for possessing small amounts of recreational drugs. In other words, many daughters wrongly assume that their fathers' generation is a bunch of uptight, conservative old guys who never did the kinds of things their daughters' generation does.

So what? What's the harm if a daughter is making the wrong assumptions about her father? The harm is this: If she believes dad is far more sexually and socially conservative than she is, she also believes that if he finds out the truth about her personal life, he will judge, criticize, or even punish her—not physically punish, but financially or emotionally punish. Expecting him to be judgmental, she certainly isn't going to him for advice or comfort. Then too, a daughter is creating unnecessary stress for herself if she is deceiving or lying to her father about things that she thinks he wouldn't approve of.

Consider Nancy's situation. She believes that her dad might refuse to help her out financially in graduate school if he finds out that she drinks and that she is sleeping with her boyfriend.

So whenever her dad comes for a visit, she races around her apartment and hides any evidence that her boyfriend sometimes spends the night: his razor, shaving lotion, brush, underwear. Then she gets rid of the beer in the fridge, hides the wine glasses, and puts the bottle of gin in the back of the linen closet so that

Checkup: Your Experiences and Beliefs

1. How do you feel about these situations: people living together before marriage, premarital sex, terminating unwanted pregnancies, gay and lesbian relationships, sex education and free contraceptives for teenagers, couples getting married because the woman is pregnant?

2. What were some of the best and worst dating experiences you've had?

3. Which romantic relationships had the greatest impact on you and how?

4. What do you wish had been different about your first romantic experiences?

5. How have your ideas about love, dating, marriage, and sex changed over the years?

6. What are some of the most romantic dates you've had?

7. Who first broke your heart and how did you recover from it?

8. What's one of the funniest things that has ever happened to you on a date?

9. What do you wish you had known about sex and love when you were younger?

10. Do you see yourself as a liberal or a conservative on social and sexual issues? Why?

dad won't know she has an occasional drink. And don't forget those birth control pills! Got to hide those too! This charade not only makes Nancy more tense when her dad is there, it makes her feel a little guilty—like a phony.

If you haven't ever discussed the topics in the "Your Experiences and Beliefs" box with each other, you're probably saying to yourself, "There is no way we're going to talk about those things—and I mean *no way!*" If that's how you feel, take a look at what daughters have to say in "The Dreaded Conversation" section. Let's figure out why you are so afraid to talk about sexual and social issues as father and daughter.

The Dreaded Conversation

Daughters who dread having a conversation with their fathers about sex or romantic relationships are often surprised by the outcomes. Consider these examples:

> "I used to think of my dad as a prude. But he told me about a time he and my mom went skinny-dipping. I just wouldn't imagine him doing something this carefree. The odd thing is that since he told me about that, I feel more relaxed talking to him about my boyfriend."

> "The really weird thing is that dad and I discovered that I'm the conservative one. I'm against abortion, against premarital sex, and against gay marriage—but he isn't. I mean, how embarrassing is that?"

> "My father is a quiet, shy man. He has never talked before about how he felt when he met my mom. But then, I had never asked him. While he was talking, I saw him as

a young man falling in love. There was tenderness in his voice I've never heard. Then he told me how scared he was to hold me when I was born and how he just cried and cried with relief because he was so worried about my mom, who had had several miscarriages. When he stopped talking, I ended up telling him the truth about why my marriage ended."

"I wasn't looking forward to this conversation. To tell the truth, I had two glasses of wine before we started talking to relax. But given what he told me about his past with women, I have begun to see my father as a person who struggles through life as a man and a husband—not just as my father."

"My dad told me about his first marriage—something my mother told me never to ask him about. But he was very open. And he said, 'Everyone needs to fumble around a little and make mistakes in order to figure out what they want and what makes them happy. You can't expect to get it right the first time—I certainly didn't.' His admitting his mistakes means I don't have to be perfect in his eyes. What a relief!"

"I was surprised when my dad talked about being hurt by women when he was a young man. I don't think of him as vulnerable or fragile in any way. He's a fairly famous surgeon; everyone is kind of intimidated by him. I had never heard him say he felt inadequate or admit his faults. Since I have always felt uncomfortable talking to my dad about personal stuff, I was surprised how easy it was after he told me his stuff."

The Fear Factor

After doing your "beliefs checkup," do the next two "fear factor checkups." A daughter often doesn't realize that her father's criticism or concerns are based on fear—fear that she will somehow get hurt. And a father often doesn't realize that his daughter's lying or refusing to discuss anything about her personal life is also based on fear—fear that he will disapprove, fear that he will somehow reject her, fear that he will love or respect her less. So use the next two quizzes to see what fears might be making your relationship less relaxed and less meaningful than it might otherwise be.

How many did you think were true? The answer is all of them.[13-14] Unfortunately, teenage daughters often don't understand the risks they face. But dad does. So when daughter starts dating and dad tries to warn her of the dangers that might lie ahead, instead of seeing him as a loving, protective ally, she sees him as a critical, judgmental intruder who doesn't trust her judgment and is interfering in her private life. On the other hand, some dads are way too fearful and overly protective because they exaggerate the risks out there for their daughter. For example, if dad believes that most teenagers are having unsafe sex with lots of people they hardly know, he's going to be overly suspicious and overly strict during his daughters' teenage years—and that's not good for the father-daughter relationship. But if dad realizes that most teenagers use contraceptives and that most wait until their older teenage years to have sex with someone they love, he will be more relaxed and take a more reasonable approach to his daughter's dating and love life.

Fathers, you might relax a little if you realize that your teenage or young adult daughter is less likely to get pregnant or to have an abortion than she would have been even a

Fathers' Fears: Teenage Sex—True or False

True or False?

_____ Nearly half of all fifteen- to nineteen-year-olds have had sex.

_____ By age fifteen, only 13 percent of teens have had sex.

_____ By age nineteen, 70 percent have had sex.

_____ Most have sex for the first time at about age seventeen.

_____ Teens are waiting longer to have sex than they did in the past.

_____ Most teenage girls have sex with a boy one to three years older than them.

_____ More than 75 percent of girls first had sex with a steady boyfriend or fiancé.

_____ Only 10 percent of girls who have sex before age twenty did so against their will.

_____ About 10 percent have oral sex but not vaginal intercourse.

_____ Almost 80 percent of teenagers used contraceptives the first time they had sex.

_____ Almost 98 percent of girls have used at least one method of birth control.

_____ About 60 percent of teenagers under eighteen say their parents know they went to a clinic for sexual checkups or contraceptives.

_____ Although fifteen- to twenty-four-year-olds are only one fourth of sexually active people, they account for nearly half of new STIs each year.

_____ Human papillomavirus (HPV) infections account for about half of their STIs.

_____ There is a vaccine to prevent HPV, which if untreated can lead to cervical cancer.

_____ Nearly a third of all teen pregnancies end in abortion.

_____ Pregnancy among black teens decreased 40 percent between 1990 and 2000.

_____ Almost 85 percent of teen pregnancies are accidental.

_____ Most teenage pregnancies are among eighteen- to nineteen-year-olds.

_____ Teen pregnancies are much higher in the United States than in other developed countries.

_____ Almost 60 percent of teenagers who have abortions do so with their parents' knowledge.

_____ **Total score** (the number you marked as "True")

decade ago.[15] Nearly half of all pregnancies in women of all ages are accidental and 40 percent in that group terminate the pregnancy. Almost 35 percent of all women will have an abortion by age forty-five. This might seem like bad news, but unwanted pregnancies and abortions are at their lowest level ever. Almost all—90 percent—of abortions occur in the first twelve weeks of the pregnancy. And almost 60 percent of women having abortions are in their twenties—60 percent of these women already have at least one child and 70 percent are poor and have never been married. So unless your daughter fits this profile, her chances of getting pregnant by accident or having an abortion are slim.

Most daughters understand that their dads are worried about them getting pregnant or contracting sexual diseases. But most don't realize dad's other fears, which are: the fear that his daughter is becoming too subservient and too dependent on her boyfriend or her husband later in her life. Dad's independent, outspoken, confident, cheerful, physically healthy daughter is turning into a wimpy, compliant, sullen, insecure little girl who lets her boyfriend or husband run the show. His daughter's strong personality and her plans for the future are shrinking instead of expanding. His daughter is pretending to be someone other than who she is to make her boyfriend happy. Dad fears that his daughter is losing herself. Unfortunately, his daughter doesn't see this; all she sees is that dad doesn't approve of the man she loves. In turn, she withdraws in anger or disappointment from her father. If only more daughters could recognize their father's fear factor—the fear that she is losing her unique self.

Assess your fear factors. Use these quizzes to discover which fears have caused each of you to misinterpret one another. Talk with each other about your fears. Come up with

three things that each of you could say or do differently to re-
duce the other's fears. You might want to look back at chapter
three for ways to make each other feel more secure during this
crucial conversation.

Daughters' Fears

Why haven't you been more open with your father
about your sexual or romantic life?

     1. _____

     2. _____

     3. _____

What do you fear losing if you were more honest with
him?

     1. _____

     2. _____

     3. _____

What would your father have to do to make it easier for
you to be more honest or more relaxed talking with him
about relationships?

     1. _____

     2. _____

     3. _____

Damaging Beliefs About Dads

Some of our fears as fathers and daughters come from the
damaging beliefs we hold about fathers. Remember what we
discussed in the second chapter: What we believe about any
group of people affects how we treat them and how we expect
them to behave toward us—even when our beliefs are not

based on reality. Here are a few of the most damaging beliefs held by both fathers and daughters:

- Fathers shouldn't talk to their daughters about love, sex, marriage, or romance.
- Fathers don't want to know anything about their daughters' personal lives.
- Fathers don't like their daughters' boyfriends because they don't want their daughters to grow up.
- Fathers aren't as wise as mothers when it comes to helping daughters with anything related to sex, romance, or love.
- Dads don't want to tell their daughters anything about their own romantic experiences.

Bravo, Dad!

"My dad invited my new boyfriend over for dinner, just the three of us. Dad cooked and wined and entertained us for four hours. His respect for my boyfriend made me feel good about myself."

"When I was getting out of a long-term relationship, my dad wrote me this letter that put everything in perspective and he called several times a week just to let me talk."

"I've always gone to my dad when I need to talk about sex or relationships. A few weeks ago, my dad sent me an email about how I need to change the way I communicate with my boyfriend. He's always been helpful that way."

"My dad has always been relaxed and open with me about sex. And because he's comfortable with it, I enjoy talking with him."

"My dad is the one who helped me realize I was in a dead-end relationship. He talked to all us girls about sex, birth control, tampons, having our periods—all of it. As a teenager, at first I was a little embarrassed, but I'm glad he did. I expect my future husband to do the same for our daughters."

"Dad always gives me good advice about my boyfriends from the guy perspective; after all, he can fill me in on all the secret stuff about men!"

"When I was in college, dad tried to have a talk with me about birth control. As amusing as it was to watch him struggle with the conversation, it was touching to see how much he cared."

"When my serious relationship ended with my long-time boyfriend, my dad sat on the couch and let me put my head in his arms while I cried and cried. He also came to me during that week when I was crying and told me to relax and everything would be fine. Even though I was just a teenager, dad never acted as if it was just "puppy love.""

"Everything Pops has ever said to me about my appearance has been positive. I was always a foot taller than other girls. But my dad encouraged me to be proud of being tall because of the advantages in sports."

Not So Bravo, Dad

"My dad has always been distant and mom is clinically depressed. I'm divorced, so I prefer random one-night stands with no attachment involved. I pick guys I feel superior to and can control. I don't trust people, especially men. I close up emotionally and never want to depend on men for anything."

"My dad sort of faded into the background when I started dating. He would meet the boys and briefly talk to them when they came over. But that was it. He never really showed much interest or asked questions. I wish he had cared more. I wanted his input and opinions. I guess I should have asked dad how he felt."

"Even though I'm almost forty, I wish sex hadn't been such a horrible taboo when I was growing up. All the more so with dad. If it hadn't seemed like such a terrible sin or if we had talked about it, I'd be better able to handle my adult sexual relationships."

"When I was a teenager, my dad walked into the room when by boyfriend and I were cuddling. Later that day, my mom said it made him uncomfortable. Since then I never felt I could hug or kiss a boy if my dad was anywhere around. I'm thirty now."

"After I started having periods, I wish my dad hadn't quit giving me a hug or kiss goodnight. He has never wanted me to have any sort of sexuality. Even though I'm married, he's made it clear that my having sex is not something he wants to think about."

[212]

"He was ruthless in criticizing my weight. I'm not comfortable with sexuality—mine or anybody else's. My dad isn't either. I think this has a lot to do with why I obsess on how I look no matter how skinny I get."

"My dad never compliments me about how I look. I wish he would, especially during times when I had no boyfriend. Even at my engagement party, he never told me I looked pretty."

"It wasn't until I was in graduate school that a girlfriend finally convinced me that having sex outside of marriage didn't make me a bad person. I never thought it made anyone else bad—just me. I got my ideas about sex from my mom. My dad is more open-minded. But he never spoke up. I wish he had."

The College Years

Many fathers worry about their daughter's sexual decisions and the men she gets involved with during her college years. As a father, you wonder: *What's my daughter up to? Is she mature enough to make wise decisions? Is she going to marry the guy she dated in college? Is she going to make mistakes that will have a negative impact on the rest of her life—getting AIDS or herpes? Having a child or getting married too young? Quitting school to get married?*

Well dads, there's good news and bad news—depending on your personal point of view. The best way to deal with the information I'm going to give you is to remind yourself that by time your daughter graduates from college, she is an adult. So whatever decisions she has been making—good or bad—are her responsibility, not yours. So let's take a look at what the majority of college women are up to.[16–17]

Dating and Hooking Up. Today on college campuses the traditional date is pretty much extinct. A man or woman might invite the other to a party, a game, or a campus event. But this isn't considered "dating." Dating is when a couple has already made a decision to be in an exclusive relationship. So if your daughter tells you she isn't dating anyone, don't assume she's lying to you. It's just that her definition of dating is different from yours.

Instead of dating, most college students are "hooking up." This means hanging out together in the dorm or running into each other at a party. At some point, the couple heads off to a dorm room or apartment where something sexual happens. Yes, they usually have been drinking. No, they're usually not drunk. Most students know each other pretty well before hooking up. So it's not likely that your daughter is going to hook up with a total stranger. "Friends with benefits" are sexually involved, but they don't think of themselves as boyfriends or girlfriends. Hooking up doesn't mean they're interested in a relationship, although that is how most serious relationships begin. So in many ways, hooking up is a lot like old-fashioned dating. As was true in their parents' generation, most college women want a serious, ongoing relationship, not a series of hook-ups year after year.

Relax, dad. Hooking up doesn't necessarily mean that your daughter is having intercourse. Many couples are just kissing and fondling—petting. Others are having oral sex or stimulating one another's genitals. Unlike their parents' generation where oral sex was considered far more intimate than intercourse, it's the reverse today. Given the fear of catching an incurable sexual disease, oral sex may be more popular than intercourse on college campuses. Although most women have some sort of sexual experience (hooking up) with more than one man during their college years, most wait to have intercourse with a man they love. Don't assume that your daughter is having risky sex with lots of men, with men she doesn't know, or with men who are taking advantage of her by getting her drunk. This is not what's going on with most college women.

Love and Marriage. What about love and marriage? What choices will your daughter probably make? Take heart, dad: Most college women are far less interested in hooking up than in having a serious, ongoing relationship with a man she loves. Yes, your daughter is likely to have a serious relationship before she graduates. And, yes, 80 percent of college women have intercourse by the time they are twenty-one. But your daughter is more likely to marry a man she meets after she graduates from college than to marry her college sweetheart. If she's like most women, she will wait until she's twenty-five or twenty-six before she gets married.

Whether your daughter is just hooking up or is in a serious relationship where she is having intercourse, odds are she isn't as sexually satisfied as the man is. Regardless of the type of sex the couple is having, the man is much more likely than the woman to have an orgasm. Why? In part because men give women less genital stimulation and less oral sex than women give men. Sometimes it's because the woman isn't willing, sometimes because the man is unwilling or inexperienced. And in part it's because a woman often pretends to have orgasms in order to make the man feel good. Unfortunately, the guy isn't getting the kind of feedback he needs in order to become a better lover.

Your Daughter's Reputation. A dad might well wonder: *Is my daughter damaging her reputation?* The bad news is that there is still a double standard. Young women who have "too

[215]

many" sexual partners or who are "too easy" do get worse reputations than men who do exactly the same things. She's likely to be considered a "slut" for the same behavior that earns the guy a reputation as a "player." College women are also more likely than men to want to be in love with the person they are sexually involved with. Although girls don't get bad reputations for having premarital sex, the double standard is still alive and well.

Love and Marriage[18]

- In 1970 most couples married at twenty-one. Today most men marry at twenty-seven and most women at twenty-five.
- In 1950 only 40 percent of college students had intercourse. Today 80 percent do.
- Most young adults who had sex before the age of eighteen say they were too young and wish they had waited.
- Most men and women marry people similar to themselves in terms of race, education, family background, and religion.
- Most young adult couples live together before they get married, and most teenagers are planning to do the same.

Dad's Sexuality

We tend to think that any tension or discomfort between fathers and daughters comes from his disapproving or feeling uncomfortable about her sexuality. But it works both ways—the adult daughter is sometimes uncomfortable with her father's sexuality or with his lifestyle.

Consider Jody's feelings: "My father and I have a very deep, loving relationship. However, since I passed from being an adolescent into a young woman, there has been something that makes me uncomfortable—middle-aged men. My dad is a nice-looking man. And he's active and athletic. He is no disgusting letch, but over the past few years, I've had an increasing discomfort around men my father's age who stare at me in a most unwelcome way. I think this has been a particularly confusing problem for me because, not so long ago, men that age were fatherly to me. Now I worry a lot that maybe my dad looks at young women my age the way that men his age look at me."

Jody is uncomfortable with the fact that her father is—or might be—a man who looks at young women in a sexually admiring way. She's upset when men her father's age stare at her because she doesn't want to believe that her dad might act this way around women her age. These men aren't saying lewd things or pushing themselves at her in any physical way, which would be inappropriate and unacceptable at any age. They're "staring" at her.

Now, it's one thing to refuse to think of our parents as sexual people when we're teenagers. But once we're adults, we should be able to accept the reality that our *fathers* and our *mothers* are sexual people. Odds are they still make love to each other. And odds are *both* of your parents occasionally "stare" at attractive young people *and attractive older people*. But there's nothing weird or unnatural about that. What Jody is trying to come to terms with is accepting her father's sexuality in the same way that fathers have to accept their daughters' sexuality.

In contrast, Ashley is comfortable with her father's sexuality. As she puts it: "He's a good-looking man, and I'm glad to see the signs that he and mom are still lovers—the way they snuggle, the way they dress up in sexy clothes and go out on dates with each other. Sure, he looks at the beautiful babes when we're at the beach. But he's never rude or gross about it. My mom looks at the guys on the beach, too. She and I actually play a game of rating the guys—like, that one is a "10" and that one is a "4." I think my brother and my dad do that too. Big deal."

As a daughter, regardless of your father's age, you might want to ask yourself these questions: Am I creating unnecessary tension in my relationship with dad by being too uptight and too judgmental about his being a sexual person? For example, do I criticize or ridicule him for wearing clothes that are too sexy (in my opinion) for a man his age? Listening to romantic or youthful music as if he was some young guy? Complimenting a woman other than my mother for looking nice? Smiling or looking at attractive women? Changing his hairstyle or growing a mustache to look more youthful? Trading in his conservative sedan for a cool sports car? Don't get me wrong; I'm not saying you should feel comfortable or that it's appropriate if your father runs around the house in his underwear or sunbathes in the nude when you're there. I'm saying that being a sexual person is nothing to be ashamed of and nothing to be criticized for—at any age.

If you are uncomfortable with your father's being a sexual person—a person who notices and appreciates attractive women of all ages—try being more open-minded. Put yourself in his place: When you're his age, do you want to be a frumpy, sexless, "old" woman who has no romance or sensuality left in her soul—a woman who can't smile or look admiringly at a younger, or older, man? Ask yourself too if you aren't being a little sexist. Do you think it's okay for your mom to notice or make comments about an attractive younger man, but it's "gross" if your dad notices good-looking women?

Don't be duped by the negative stereotypes about older people's sexuality. Underlying the supposedly funny jokes about "dirty old men" are two insulting messages that might be affecting the way you treat your dad. First, there is something weird, laughable, or unnatural about older men—our fathers or grandfathers—having sexual feelings or noticing and appreciating beautiful women. Second, older women—our mothers and grandmothers—are "superior" to men in that they never have sexual feelings or notice and appreciate good-looking men. What nonsense!

Your Father's Sexuality

Are dad and grandpa "dirty old men" or are they men who still have romance in their souls and want to remain younger than spring?

> "Beautiful girls, walk a little slower when you walk by me.
> Lingering sunsets, stay a little longer with the lonely sea.
> And let the music play, as long as there's a song to sing.
> And I will stay younger than spring."
>
> —Lyrics from "This Is All I Ask"
> by Gordon Jenkins (1956)

Privacy or Deception?

Am I saying that fathers and daughters should tell each other everything about their sexual lives? Or that they should share the details of their romantic lives with each other? *Absolutely not!* Do you remember the discussion we had in an earlier chapter about the difference between privacy and deception? Privacy is good for father-daughter relationships—lies, secrecy, and deception are not. Lying about who you are and what you believe is different from respecting each other's privacy.

Let's consider Beth and her dad, George, who have gotten themselves into a pickle because they have been deceiving each other for so long. Both justified deceiving the other with, "I'm just protecting my privacy." Beth has been dating Ben for two years and is now engaged to him. Although her dad has talked to Ben on the phone many times, they have never met because Beth and her dad live so far away from each other. Now her dad is finally coming to visit his future son-in-law and to talk about the wedding plans. The one thing Beth hasn't told her dad is that Ben's skin isn't the same color as hers. They are an interracial couple who will have an interracial marriage and raise interracial kids—and dad isn't going to be happy about any of this news.

As for her dad, he has a little secret of his own—a secret he's been hiding from Beth since he and her mother divorced ten years ago. Now that he and Beth will be talking about her wedding plans, he wonders what he's going to do about his "friend" Steve. Although dad often talks to Beth about his good friend Steve, he hasn't told her that they have lived together for many years and that they are "more than friends." If only this father and daughter hadn't confused privacy with deception! And, yes, this is a true story.

Dad's Approval

I've found that the adult daughter who desperately wants her father to approve of her sexual or romantic decisions generally has the least confidence about the decisions she has made for herself. Because she is ambivalent, she wants her father to vote "yes"—not only to boost her confidence, but also to reassure herself that she's making the right decisions. But when dad votes "undecided," daughter is no happy camper.

Take Sandy and her father Tim, for example. She just got engaged, but her dad doesn't seem very enthusiastic. As Sandy puts it, "Sure, it would be nice if dad was jumping up and down for joy, but I'm not wiped out about it. I know that this is right for me. Eventually dad will see that, too. Why should I hassle him just because he'd like me to wait until I'm a little older to get married?" As her father says, "I know Sandy wants me to be as excited about this as she is. I don't have anything against her fiancé. I just wish she'd wait another year or so until she's paid off her debts and gets more settled in her new job. But my daughter and I don't play games with each other. We don't do any phony pretending stuff. We're honest with each other. And that's what matters."

In contrast, Joyce is furious with her father because he isn't excited about her getting married. She says, "Dad is being a total jerk! If he really loved me, he would be as happy as I am. He's ruining everything for me. He actually had the nerve to ask if I thought Joe was the right guy for me. Can you believe that?" But as her dad, Randy, puts it, "My daughter has been through this sort of thing before. She jumps into relationships pretty quickly and then gets her heart broken. Just last month she was saying she wasn't sure this new fellow was right for her. And now they're engaged. How did she expect me to react?"

When it comes to the daughter's decisions about her romantic life, remember the old adage: "You made your bed. Now lie in it." In other words, after her teenage years, a daughter is old enough to live with the choices she makes about the men in her life—and the wise father realizes this. As a daughter, you have to accept this responsibility, rather than acting like a little girl who wants "daddy" to applaud your decisions. As a father, you have to accept the fact that, even when you worry that she might end up getting hurt, your daughter is a woman who needs to be "making her own bed and lying in it."

Handling Your Differences

As father and daughter, you probably aren't going to see eye to eye on every issue having to do with sex or social issues. The important question is: How can you prevent your differences from hurting your father-daughter relationship? I suggest you both ARM yourselves: Accept, Reassure, Mail.

Accept each other. By accept, I mean do not try to change each other's opinions and do *not* seek the other's approval. Instead, seek and give acceptance. As we've discussed in an earlier chapter, acceptance and approval are two entirely different things. *Accepting* someone means that, even though we don't agree with some of the choices they have made or some of their beliefs, we continue to love them and to treat them with respect. We don't try to make the person feel guilty or ashamed. We don't allow our differences to damage our relationship.

Many fathers and daughters say they can't "accept" the other's beliefs or choices because "that means I'm giving up my principles. I'm turning my back on what I believe in." Well, no, that's not what acceptance means. Acceptance doesn't mean you *approve* of the other's person's choices—or that you abandon the principles by which you live your life. Acceptance means you don't keep badgering the other person to give up their principles and adopt yours or force the other to prove that they love or respect you by applauding or agreeing with your decisions. For example, dad, you can *accept* your daughter's decision to live with her boyfriend even though you have told her that you don't *approve* and don't agree with her. And daughter, you can *accept* your father's decision not to have you and your boyfriend share a bedroom together in his home even though you have told him you don't *approve* and don't agree with him.

For the sake of your relationship, after you've discussed your beliefs and the decisions you're making in your personal life, *let it go*. Don't behave like contestants on debate teams trying to win points. You're both adults who have formed your own opinions about how to live your private life. Given your age, neither of you is likely to be won over by some brilliant argument that the other puts forth. If either of you eventually changes your opinion, it's probably not because of those heated debates you've had with each other.

Reassure each other. What's often happening is that you both want to feel loved and respected. And you believe the other person has to show love and respect by agreeing with what you have decided to do. Maybe you believe that loving and respecting someone means doing what he or she wants you to do in your personal life. Not so! We all have friends, family, and spouses that we love and respect but whose lifestyles and personal choices differ from ours. Fathers and daughters are no exception. Reassure each other that, even though you don't agree, you still love and respect each other. As trivial as this sounds, try saying things like, "Even though we can't agree on this, what matters most is that we love and respect each other." Or, "Just because I don't agree with you on this doesn't mean I love or respect you any less."

Mail (literally send mail). Many fathers and daughters find that writing a letter or sending an email makes it easier to discuss "it"—that one situation or topic that you've been dreading having to talk about. Especially if you have never discussed "it" or have tried but failed miserably, mail can be the best way to start. Remember though: Don't stoop to emotional blackmail. Steer clear of the FOG: Fear, Obligation, Guilt.

A Father from the Old Country

What advice would you give Juanita and her father, Luis?

Luis: *"My daughter no longer respects me. She has turned her back on what our religion teaches. She doesn't ever want to be a mother. She just told me that she has been living with a man for the last five years. This is a sin. By accident, I found out that she had an abortion six years ago. It is like she is spitting in my face. I have wasted all these years trying to teach her the right ways to live. If I am true to my religious beliefs, how can I ever invite her and that man to my home? I have failed as a father."*

Juanita: *"I love my father. But the beliefs he grew up with in his country are not ones I can live by. I was raised in the States. I'm thirty-five years old. I have an exciting, demanding career that I love. Lots of travel. It's great. I don't want kids—not now, not ever. I've lied to my father for years about my private life. But finally, I had to tell him that my boyfriend and I have been living together for six years because we're buying a house together. And I'm tired of feeling guilty lying to him. Now he's so angry that he won't even come to the phone to talk to me."*

Moving Forward

It's been said that "what we *choose* to focus on enlarges." So if either of you chooses to focus on the differences between your social or sexual lifestyles, you are choosing to enlarge the gap in your father-daughter relationship. But if you choose to focus on what brings you joy together, you enlarge that joy. My hope is that both of you are loving and wise enough to allow each other to live your personal lives according to your own beliefs—and to focus on what you love about your father-daughter relationship rather than on issues that could divide you.

Reconciling
or Letting Go

9

❖

Barriers to Reconciling

Throughout this book we've looked at ways to strengthen or to rebuild your relationship in situations where the two of you had a relationship with each other throughout most of the daughter's childhood. But in millions of families, dad wasn't part of his daughter's life while she was growing up. While there are many reasons why these dads "disappear" from or move to the margins of their daughters' lives, some of the most common are having children out of wedlock, living in poverty, and spending time in prison, usually for drug-related crimes. Although these problems affect all races, African American dads and daughters are hardest hit.[1-3] Regardless of your race, if dad wasn't part of his daughter's life while she was growing up, your bond was seriously damaged—or destroyed altogether.

As the dad or as the daughter, you may be thinking about reconciling—or just meeting each other again. Except in cases where the father has been sexually or physically abusive, there are ways to reconnect even after years apart. By reconnect I don't mean that most of these fathers and daughters end up with a close relationship for the remainder of their lives. But many are glad they made the effort to get together before time ran out. So let's see how they started the process.

Barriers for Black Dads and Daughters

- Nearly half of all prisoners are black men and 30 percent of black men spend time in jail at some point in their lives.[4]
- Black children are nine times more likely than white children to have a father in prison.[5]
- 80 percent of African American daughters spend a large part of their childhood living apart from their dads and 70 percent are born to unmarried parents.[6]
- The majority of unmarried parents' relationships end within the first few years after their child is born.[7]

Dads Who Leave, Daughters Who Grieve

Regardless of what separated you as father and daughter, the outcome is usually the same: Dads leave—daughters grieve. Many fathers may think their grown-up daughters have gotten over not having had a dad in their lives. Not so! As a father, maybe you still don't realize the price your daughter paid for your absence. But as a daughter, you know. Having grown up without a father herself, Jonetta Rose Barras describes what happens to most fatherless daughters:[8, 9]

- Feeling fundamentally unlovable and unworthy of a man's love.
- Choosing men who are married or otherwise can't commit to a relationship.
- Feeling that you never quite measure up.
- Feeling that you always have to be in control—especially in relationships with men.
- Continually searching for a man to give you what dad didn't give.
- Looking for love through meaningless or promiscuous sex.
- Feeling unresolved pain that resurfaces every time a relationship ends.
- Comforting yourself by abusing drugs, alcohol, or food.
- Being unable to trust men enough to create a stable relationship.
- Feeling extremely angry and resentful toward men in general.
- Suffering from clinical depression.
- Acting like a super woman who can handle everything without anyone's help.
- Feeling that most men—especially fathers—are no good.
- Having a baby at an early age in an attempt to feel loved.
- Choosing men who aren't good to you or good for you.
- Being extremely needy or overly dependent on men.
- Feeling that you have to be nearly perfect before a man can love you.
- Leaving a decent relationship instead of working

through the problems because you assume he's going to leave you anyway.

• Feeling that you have to earn love or change things about yourself because you're not lovable enough just the way you are.

Let's face it: most women probably feel and behave this way sometimes, even when they have spectacular relationships with their fathers. But women who have grown up without their fathers feel and behave this way *most* of the time throughout *most* of their lives. Jonetta Barras believes that black daughters are more likely to suffer in these ways because society makes them feel they're not quite good enough or attractive enough by white standards: "Your hair is too nappy, your butt too wide, your nose not pointed enough, and your lips too full."[10] And on top of that, your father abandoned you.

Dads Who Leave, Daughters Who Grieve

"I met my father for the first time when I was thirty-seven years old. I felt joy at the prospect of having a father. But I was equally confused about how I should respond to this new opportunity. One part of me argued that I didn't need him after all these years. Another part of me longed to reach out to him, have him envelop me in his arms and say he loved me—that he had always loved me—and missed me terribly during all those years of separation. But our reunion was too brief for any real healing or bonding to take place. I became peeved at a perceived slight, and I moved away from him. He died two years after our initial meeting."

—Jonetta Rose Barras[11]

"I can't imagine what was powerful enough to pull him away from me. Did he move on to the next woman or relationship? Was it the nightlife that was so compelling? Was it his singing career that made having a family so unattractive? Did he think about me when he walked away? Did he think so little of me that it was easy to leave? Did he think so little of himself that he felt he had nothing to contribute? Why?"

—Robin Wright King[12]

"Men are not objects for me to conquer. All men are not dogs. Women are not trinkets to be played with. And as women, we do not have to stoop below ourselves because our hearts have been broken. I have played the role of dog, bitch, pimp, and warrior as a defense mechanism and survivor of childhood trauma. My daddy broke my heart at a very young age, and it has taken years for me to reconcile that."

—Tina Fakhrid-Deen[13]

"Upon reaching adulthood the wish to have a relationship with my father has waned slightly. I am no longer curious to know what this man was/is like. I no longer wish to know which of my features resembles his. I no longer wish to know how he was/is like mentally in order to understand my depressive episodes. I also no longer wish to thank him for my pretty feet that I know, without a doubt, came from him. I no longer wish to thank him for being part of my creation. I no longer wish these things…I want them."

—Nkiru Nso-Ani[14]

"After a twelve-year hiatus, I didn't recognize him at first. The long Jheri curl of his youth was replaced with a gray, slightly balding crew cut. He hugged me tight and whispered in my ear, "I love you once, I love you twice, I love you more than beans and rice." So, he remembered. It was the last thing I'd ever said to him, written in a letter to the jail. I was about eleven years old then."

—Tina Smith Walker[15]

Dads Who Grieve*

"My daughter has been estranged from me for nearly seven years now. She refuses to see me or talk with me. I have racked my brain as to the reason, but can find no logical answer. I started a journal for my daughter before she was born. If she never reconciles with me, she will at least have the words that I write to tell her how much I love her. I hope that before my time expires, she will find peace with me; even if it's for a brief period of time, I will once again find the love we had when she was younger."

"My daughter doesn't want me in her life. I can only love her from a distance. What I have learned through all this is that it doesn't matter how much I love her if she won't receive it. But I will never give up hope or stop loving her. Even though she doesn't love me, I hope she will find love in her life and will have much happiness."

"There are no words to describe the devastation and agony of my daughter not letting me be part of her life.

---

* From fathers' emails and letters to Dr. Nielsen

She even returned the gifts I mailed to her kids for Christmas – unopened. I'm desperately searching for a tool kit to fix our relationship. But after all these years, even now as a grandfather I don't know how to stop the aching."

"I think I have forgiven myself for not being as good a father as I should have been. But then I fall apart and feel guilty all over again whenever I see fathers and daughters laughing together – or when I think of my daughter getting married without my being there. I long for the day when my daughter will answer my phone calls or letters."

So Now What?

If you're a dad who wasn't in your daughter's life while she was growing up, you have probably grieved, too. Your suffering doesn't get much attention in our society because most men don't talk about their pain. So it's easy to assume that absent dads just move on without ever thinking about the children they left behind. That may be true for some. But many absent fathers do feel the pain—sometimes for a lifetime.[16–18]

Still, because your daughter was only a child when you disappeared or moved to the margins of her life, you can't expect her to understand the reasons why you left—or to sympathize with you—or to forgive you automatically if you contact her. From her perspective, you *chose* to abandon her, turned your back on her—stopped loving her. And that's done, finished, over. You can't erase the past. But you can do something now. First you can accept this reality: *Even though she's grown up and hasn't seen you for years, she probably still feels this way—that you don't love her and don't want her in your life.* It's time to man up. Get in touch with her. Explain. Apologize. Ask her to forgive you, if not now, then maybe after she gets to know you better. Ask her to let you play some part in her life—whatever part *she* chooses. If you need help getting started, see the sample letter on page 192.

As a daughter, you have two choices. You can either keep on doing what you're doing now: not contacting your dad or refusing to see him if he tries to get in touch with you. Or you can reach out and give things a chance. But how? The wisest and most practical advice I've ever read comes from Jonetta Rose Barras in *Bridges: Reuniting Daughters and Daddies*. You owe it to yourself to read both of her books. Here's a brief summary of her advice:

- When you get together, admit how much pain you have been in. Speak it out loud.
- Don't spend your time blaming each other or blaming others for what happened.
- Don't rely on what others have told you about what happened in your family in the past. Explore the past together by sharing your stories.
- Name a few specific things that each of you will have to do to start rebuilding.
- Set reasonable goals.
- Decide what each of you can do now to ease some of the pain from the past.
- Go slowly. Don't expect sudden changes.
- Initially don't unload all your bad feelings or talk about the heavy stuff.
- Tell each other specifically what it is you want from your relationship from here on—not something vague like "love me" but something specific like "Talk to each other regularly and spend time together at least once a month."

- Tell each other what you think you can contribute to him/her from here on.
- If either of you decides that you don't want to keep trying to build a relationship, tell the other person. *Whatever you do, don't just disappear, stop phoning, or refuse to respond to a letter or call.*

As a daughter, try to put aside some of the bad stories you've heard about your dad. You may think you know why things fell apart between your parents or why he withdrew from your life. Odds are you've heard your mother's side many times. But you probably haven't heard your dad's. Now that you're older, you're in a better position to re-examine the past. As they say, there are *three* sides to every story! Remember too, that some dads and daughters are able to restore their bond, even after years of absence—for example, Oprah and her father.

Oprah's Dad

By time she turned fifteen, Oprah had already had a miscarriage, was doing poorly in school, and had a troubled relationship with her single mother. Her parents, who were never married, had separated when she was young. With her life in a mess at the age of fifteen, she went to live with her father, Vernon, a barber in Tennessee, and his wife. Oprah credits her dad for turning her life around. With his strict rules and loving guidance, she excelled in school— and in life! At seventeen she became a radio broadcaster and from there on her career soared. In 1987, she endowed ten scholarships at Tennessee State University in her father's honor.[19]

Are you afraid? Nervous? That's okay. As Barras explains, you are afraid of three things: of being rejected, of being abandoned again, and of making a commitment to each other. Are you already making up excuses for why you can't contact each other? Okay, then ask yourself: *What have I got to lose?* You don't have a relationship now—if things don't work out, you're probably not going to end up feeling worse than you do now.

Are you going to be able to build the kind of relationship you always dreamed of? Maybe. Maybe not. For sure you're not going to create the "daddy's little girl" connection that you both needed in the past. You're both adults now—your goal is to create an adult bond.

Is being part of each other's lives going to erase all the pain about the past, to magically transform your life into something incredibly wonderful? No. That's make-believe, not real life. But reconnecting can soothe a lot of old wounds and dowse the fires of anger. Does getting together mean you have to forget all the painful things that happened in the past? No. It just means you stop punishing the other person for those mistakes and you allow yourself to enjoy whatever you have to offer each other from here on. Is there a chance that things just won't work out? Sure. But you'll never catch a fish if you don't throw your line in the water.

Notes

Chapter 2

1. Associated Press, "Fatherhood Activists Call On Verizon," *Winston-Salem Journal*, May 15, 2004, p. A5.
2. N. Barnett and C. Rivers, *Same Difference: How Gender Myths Hurt Our Relationships*, Basic Books, New York, 2004.
3. A. Gates, "Men on Television," *New York Times*, April 9, 2000, p. 2.
4. R. Marin, "Fathers Eat Best" *New York Times*, February 6, 2005, p. ST2.
5. R. Devlin, *Relative Intimacy: Fathers, Adolescent Daughters and Modern Culture*, University of North Carolina, Chapel Hill, 2005.
6. M. Stetz, "Hollywood Fathers and Daughters," *Literature and Film Quarterly*, Vol. 35, 2007, pp. 116–32.
7. I. Nash, *American Sweethearts*, New York University Press, New York, 2005.
8. Atwood Associates, "Father's Day Cards," Survey for Hallmark Cards, 2005.
9. R. LeRossa and C. Jaret, "Mother's Day and Father's Day Comic Strips," *Sex Roles*, Vol. 56, 2001, pp. 693–18.
10. S. Flannery, "Fatherhood in American Children's Literature," *Fathering*, Vol. 4, 2006, pp. 71–95.
11. National Fatherhood Initiative, "Pop's Culture: Survey of Dads' Attitudes on Fathering," National Fatherhood Initiative, Gaithersburg, MD, 2006.
12. Roper Poll, "Dads Talk About Their Daughters," United Business Media for Dads and Daughters, Minneapolis, MN, 2004.
13. K. Pruett, *Fatherneed*, Broadway Books, New York, 2001.
14. D. Eyer, *Mother Infant Bonding: A Scientific Fiction*, Yale University, New Haven, CT, 1994.

15. S. Hardy, *Mother Nature*, Ballantine, New York, 1999.

16. S. Hays, *The Cultural Contradictions of Motherhood*, Yale University, New Haven, CT, 2008.

17. W. Farrell, *Father and Child Reunion*, Tarcher, New York, 2001.

18. R. Palkovitz, *Involved Fathering and Men's Adult Development*, Erlbaum, London, 2002.

19. N. Townsend, *The Package Deal*, Temple University, Philadelphia, 2003.

20. Radcliff Policy Center, *Life's Work*, Radcliff University, Radcliff Policy Center, Cambridge, MA, 2000.

21. M. Lamb, *Role of the Father in Child Development*, Wiley, New York, 2004.

22. E. Flouri, *Fathering and Child Outcomes*, John Wiley, Sussex, England, 2005.

23. C. Tarnis and N. Cabrera, *Handbook of Father Involvement*, Lawrence Erlbaum, New York, 2002.

24. T. Wilson, *Strangers to Ourselves*, Knopf, New York, 2002.

25. D. McAdams, *The Redemptive Self*, Crown, New York 2007.

26. T. Wilson, *Strangers to Ourselves*, Knopf, New York, 2002.

27. L. Perosa, "Identity Development in Young Adult Women," *Journal of Adolescent Research*, Vol. 17, 2002, pp. 235–58.

28. B. Bates, J. Dodge, and K. Ellis, "Father Absence and Teenage Pregnancy," *Child Development*, Vol. 74, 2003, pp. 801–21.

29. M. Meeker, *Strong Fathers, Strong Daughters*, Ballantine, New York, 2007.

30. L. Siegel and B. Welsh, *Juvenile Delinquency*. Belmont, CA: Wadsworth Publishers, 2008

31. M. Maine, *Father Hunger: Fathers, Daughters and the Pursuit of Thinness*, Gurze, New York, 2004.

32. R. Agras, "Fathers Influence on Daughters Eating Disorders," *Journal of the American Academy of Child and Adolescent Psychiatry*, Vol. 115, 2007, pp. 234–39.

33. J. Trowell, *The Importance of Fathers*, Brunner-Routledge, New York, 2002.

34. M. Murdock, *Fathers' Daughters*, Springer Journal, New York, 2005.

35. J. Fullinwider, "Transition to Adulthood: Female Identity Development," *Family Process*, Vol. 32, 2006, pp. 87–103.

36. L. Leonard, *The Wounded Woman: Healing the Father-Daughter Wound*, Shambahla, Boston, 1998.

37. Tarnis, C. and N. Cabrera, *Handbook of Father Involvement*. New York: Lawrence Erlbaum, 2002.

38. D. Jack, *Cultural Perspectives on Women's Depression*, Oxford University Press, Oxford, England, 2008.

39. S. Brotherson and J. White, *Why Fathers Count*, Men's Studies Press, Harriman, TN, 2006.

40. E. Washington, "Daughters Influence Fathers," *Economics Journal*, Vol. 45, 2007, pp. 45–46.

41. S. Greenblatt, *Will in the World: William Shakespeare*, Norton, New York, 2004.

42. G. Gawalt and A. Gawalt, *First Daughters*, Black Dog & Leventhal, New York, 2004.

43. S. Jayson "Like Daughter, Like Father?" *USA Today*, June 17, 2007, p. B21.

44. Ibid.

45. B. Glassner, *The Culture of Fear: Why Americans Are Afraid of the Wrong Things*, Basic Books, New York, 2000.

46. J. Katz, *The Macho Paradox*, Sourcebooks, Naperville, IL, 2006.

47. E. Smith, *Race, Sport and the American Dream*, Carolina Academic Press, Durham, NC, 2007.

48. T. Alexander, *Diary of a Tired Black Man*, Screen Time Films, 2006.

49. K. Taylor, *Black Fathers*, Doubleday, New York, 2003.

50. O. Clayton, R. Mincy, and W. Blankenhorn, *Black Fathers in Contemporary Society*, Russell Sage, New York, 2006.

51. M. Connor and J. White, *Black Fathers: An Invisible Presence in America*, Lawrence Erlbaum, New York, 2006.

52. R. Vassel, *Daughters of Men: African American Women and Their Fathers*, Amistad, New York, 2007.

53. M. Perchinske, *Commitment: Fatherhood in Black America*, University of Missouri, Columbia, MO, 1998.

54. Ibid.

55. C. Ross, *Pops: Celebration of Black Fathers*, Stuart, Taboori & Chang, New York, 2007.

56. Ibid.

57. S. Colbert and V. Harrison, *Color Him Father: Stories of Love and Rediscovery of Black Men*, Kinship Press, Philadelphia, 2006.

Chapter 3

1. D. Goleman, *Emotional Intelligence*, Bantam, New York, 2005.

2. Ibid.

3. H. Gardner, *Multiple Intelligences*, Perseus, New York, 2006.

4. M. Kimmel, *Manhood in America*, Allyn Bacon, Boston, 2006.

5. M. Maine, *Father Hunger: Fathers, Daughters and the Pursuit of Thinness*, Gurze, New York, 2004.

6. S. Bowling and R. Werner, "Father Daughter Relationships and Adolescent Female Sexuality," *Journal of HIV/AIDS Prevention*, Vol. 3, 2000, pp. 5–28.

7. M. Hutchinson, "Communication Between Parents and Daughters on Sexual Risk Behaviors," *Family Relations*, Vol. 51, 2002, pp. 238–47.

8. M. Miller, "Parent Adolescent Communication," *Journal of Adolescent Research*, Vol. 17, 2002, pp. 604–16.

9. R. Rotta and R. Dumlao, "Communication Between Fathers and Daughters," Health Communications, Vol. 14, 2002, pp. 199–19.

10. N. Way and D. Gillman, "Adolescent Girls' Perceptions of Their Fathers," *Journal of Early Adolescence*, Vol. 20, 2000, pp. 309–31.

11. L. Nielsen, "College Daughters' Relationships with Their Fathers: A Fifteen Year Study," *College Student Journal*, Vol. 54, 2006, pp. 16–30.

12. C. Simon, *Fatherless Women*, Wiley, New York, 2001.

13. V. Secunda, *Losing Your Parents, Finding Yourself*, Random House, New York, 2000.

14. K. Patterson, J. Grenny, R McMillan, and A. Switzler, *Crucial Conversations*, McGraw Hill, New York, 2002.

15. R. LeRossa and C. Jaret, "Mother's Day and Father's Day Comic Strips," *Sex Roles*, Vol. 56, 2001, pp. 693–18.

16. Atwood Associates, "Father's Day Cards," Hallmark Cards, 2005.

17. Associated Press, "Fatherhood Activists Call on Verizon," *Winston Salem Journal*, 2004, May 15, A5.

18. N. Barnett and C. Rivers, *Same Difference: How Gender Myths Hurt Our Relationships*, Basic Books, New York, 2004.

19. M. Stetz, "Hollywood Fathers and Daughters," *Literature and Film Quarterly*, Vol. 35, 2007, pp 116–32.

20. L. Lee, "Another Dad Flick and Guys Are Crying," *New York Times*, December 29, 2002, B15.

21. E. Flouri, *Fathering and Child Outcomes*, John Wiley, Sussex, England, 2005.

22. M. Lamb, *Role of the Father in Child Development*, Wiley, New York, 2004.

23. S. Forward, *Emotional Blackmail*, Harper Collins, New York, 1998.

Chapter 4

1. C. Ahrons, "Family Ties After Divorce," *Family Process*, Vol. 46, 2006, pp. 53–65.

2. V. Bengston and R. Roberts, *How Fathers Still Matter*, Cambridge Press, New York, 2002.

3. L. Nielsen, "College Daughters' Relationships with Their Fathers: A Fifteen Year Study," *College Student Journal*, Vol. 54, 2006, pp. 16–30.

4. M. Scott, A. Booth, and V. King, "Post Divorce Father-Adolescent Closeness," *Journal of Marriage and Family*, Vol. 69, 2007, pp. 1194–1209.

5. M. Miller, "Parent Adolescent Communication," *Journal of Adolescent Research*, Vol. 17, 2002, pp. 604–16.

6. V. Secunda, *Losing Your Parents, Finding Yourself*, Random House, New York, 2000.

7. C. Simon, *Fatherless Women*, Wiley, New York, 2001.

8. M. Lamb, *Role of the Father in Child Development*, Wiley, New York, 2004.

9. J. Pleck, "Men in Families" in M. Lamb, *The Role of the Father in Child Development*, Wiley, New York, 2004, pp. 222–71.

10. R. Devlin, *Relative Intimacy: Fathers, Adolescent Daughters and Modern Culture*, University of North Carolina, Chapel Hill, 2005.

11. S. Flannery, "Fatherhood in American Children's Literature," *Fathering*, Vol. 4, 2006, pp. 71–95.

12. I. Nash, *American Sweethearts*, New York University Press, New York, 2005.

13. M. Stetz, "Hollywood Fathers and Daughters," Literature and Film Quarterly, Vol. 35, 2007, pp. 116–32.

14. D. Merkin, "The Public Father," *New York Times Magazine*, March 20, 2000, p 58.

15. S. Muir, *The Book of Telling*, Schocken, New York, 2005.

16. S. Miller, *Story of My Father*, Random House, New York, 2004.

17. C. Nickson, *Mariah Carey Revisited*, St. Martins, New York, 1998.

18. E. Williams and W. Stadiem, *Dear Senator: A Memoir by the Daughter of Strom Thurmond*, Regan Books, New York, 2005.

19. J. Cross, *Secret Daughter: A Mixed Race Daughter and the Mother Who Gave Her Away*, Penguin, New York, 2007.

20. L. Funderburg, *Pig Candy: Taking My Father South*, Free Press, New York, 2008.

Chapter 5

1. M. Messner and M. Kimmel, Men's Lives, Allyn Bacon, Boston, 2006.

2. R. Palkovitz, *Involved Fathering and Men's Adult Development*, Erlbaum, London, 2002.

3. N. Townsend, *The Package Deal*, Temple University, Philadelphia, 2003.

4. J. Troilo and M. Coleman, "College Students Perceptions of Father Stereotypes," *Marriage and the Family*, Vol. 70, 2008, pp. 218–27.

5. R. Caputo, "Adult Daughters as Parental Caregivers," *Journal of Economic Issues*, Vol. 23, 2002, pp. 83–97.

6. S. Coontz, *History of Marriage*, Penguin, New York, 2007.

7. Census Bureau, "Income and Educational Attainment," Department of Labor, Washington, DC, 2007.

8. N. Barnett, "The Dual Earner Family" in M. Halpern's *Tilting the Scale on Work-Family Balance*, Erlbaum, Mahway, New Jersey, 2007, pp. 145–57.

9. P. England, C. Beaulieu, and M. Ross, "Women's Employment," *Gender and Society*, Vol. 18, 2004, pp. 494–509.

10. N. Dowd, *Redefining Fatherhood*, Harcourt, Brace, Jovanovich, New York, 2000.

11. R. Devlin, *Relative Intimacy: Fathers, Adolescent Daughters and Modern Culture*, University of North Carolina, Chapel Hill, 2005.

12. F.W.I., "Family and Work Trends," *Family & Work Institute*, New York, 2007.

13. Ibid.

14. Ibid.

15. J. Hill, "Studying Working Fathers," *Fathering*, Vol. 15, 2003, pp. 239–62.

16. M. Milke, "The Time Squeeze," *Journal of Marriage and Family*, Vol. 66, 2004, pp. 739–61.

17. N. Cabrera et al., "Fatherhood in the Twenty First Century," *Child Development*, Vol. 71, 2003, pp. 127–36.

18. J. Pleck, "Men in Families," in M. Lamb (ed.), *The Role of the Father in Child Development*, Wiley, New York, 2004, pp. 222–71.

19. P. Amato and A. Booth, *Alone Together: How Marriage in America Is Changing*, Harvard University Press, Cambridge, MA, 2006.

20. Radcliff Policy Center, "Life's Work," Radcliff Policy Center, Radcliff University, Cambridge, MA, 2000.

21. O. Sullivan, *Changing Gender Relations, Changing Families*, Rowman & Littlefield, New York, 2006.

22. M. Sunstrom and A. Duvander, "Childcare and Parental Leave in Sweden," *European Sociological Review*, Vol. 18, 2004, p. 447.

23. S. Bianchi, J. Robinson, and M. Milkie, *Changing Rhythms of the American Family*, Sage, New York, 2006.

24. Ibid.

25. Ibid.
26. L. Cooke, "Doing Gender in Context," *Journal of Sociology*, Vol. 112, 2006, pp. 442–72.
27. R. Barnett and K. Gareis, "Shiftwork and Parenting Behaviors," *Journal of Family Issues*, Vol. 28, 2007, pp. 727–48.
28. K. Gerson, "Moral Dilemmas, Moral Strategies, and the Transformation of Gender," *Gender & Society*, Vol. 16, 2007, pp. 8–28.
29. M. Kimmel, *Manhood in America*, Allyn Bacon, Boston, 2006.
30. O. Clayton, S. Mintz, and D. Blankenhorn, ed. *Black Fathers in Contemporary Society*, Russell Sage Foundation, New York, 2003.
31. E. Spragins, "Loans From Parents," *New York Times*, March 3, 2002.
32. V. Marino, "The $249,180 Childhood," *New York Times*, February 9, 2003.
33. A Robbin and A. Wilner, *Quarterlife Crisis*, Tarcher, Los Angeles, 2008.
34. K. Frist, *Love You, Daddy Boy*, Taylor, New York, 2006.

Chapter 6
1. V. Bengston and R. Roberts, *How Families Still Matter*, Cambridge Press, New York, 2002.
2. M. Miller, "Parent Adolescent Communication," *Journal of Adolescent Research*, Vol. 17, 2002, pp. 604–16.
3. L. Nielsen, "College Daughters' Relationships with Their Fathers: A Fifteen Year Study," *College Student Journal*, Vol. 54, 2006, pp. 16–30.
4. M. Scott, A. Booth, and V. King, "Post Divorce Father-Adolescent Closeness," *Journal of Marriage and Family*, Vol. 69, 2007, pp. 1194–1209.
5. J. Suitor and K. Pillemer, "Why Mothers Favor Adult Daughters Over Sons," *Sociological Perspectives*, Vol. 49, 2006, pp. 139–61.
6. Associated Press, "Fatherhood Activists Call On Verizon," *Winston-Salem Journal*, May 15, 2004, A5.
7. S. Flannery, "Fatherhood in American Children's Literature," *Fathering*, Vol. 4, 2006, pp. 71–95.
8. A. Gates, "Men on Television," *New York Times*, April 9, 2000, p. 2.
9. R. LeRossa and C. Jaret, "Mother's Day and Father's Day Comic Strips," *Sex Roles*, Vol. 56, 2001, pp. 693–718.
10. A. Stanley, "On TV Men Are the New Women," *New York Times*, September 28, 2003.
11. R. Marin, "Father Eats Best," *New York Times*, February 6, 2005, p. ST2.
12. M. Stetz, "Hollywood Fathers and Daughters," *Literature and Film Quarterly*, Vol. 35, 2007, pp.116–32.

13. R. Devlin, *Relative Intimacy: Fathers, Adolescent Daughters and Modern Culture*, University of North Carolina, Chapel Hill, 2005.
14. I. Nash, *American Sweethearts*, New York University Press, New York, 2005.
15. N. Barnett and C. Rivers, *Same Difference: How Gender Myths Hurt Our Relationships*, Basic Books, New York 2004.
16. K. Dindia and D. Canary, *Sex Differences and Similarities in Communication*, Erlbaum, Mahway, New Jersey, 2006.
17. H.H.S., "Child Maltreatment Report," U.S. Department of Health and Human Services, Youth and Families, Washington, DC, 2003.
18. B. Ogilvie, *Mother-Daughter Incest*, Haworth, New York 2004.
19. D. Eyer, *Mother Infant Bonding: A Scientific Fiction*, Yale University Press, New Haven, CT, 1994.
20. S. Hardy, *Mother Nature*, Ballantine, New York, 1999.
21. H. Goldenberg and I. Goldenberg, *Family Therapy*, Brooks Cole, New York, 2007.
22. P. Titelman, *Triangles: Bowen Family Systems Perspectives*, Haworth, New York, 2007.
23. H. Goldenberg and I. Goldenberg, *Family Therapy*, Brooks Cole, New York, 2007.
24. P. Titelman, *Triangles: Bowen Family Systems Perspectives*, Haworth, New York, 2007.
25. Census Bureau, "Income and Educational Attainment," Department of Labor, Washington, DC, 2007.
26. F.W.I., "Family and Work Trends," Family & Work Institute, New York, 2007.
27. J. Pleck, "Men in Families" in M. Lamb (ed.), *The Role of the Father in Child Development*, Wiley, New York, 2004, pp. 222–71.
28. O. Sullivan, *Changing Gender Relations, Changing Families*, Rowman & Littlefield, New York, 2006.
29. P. Amato and A. Booth, *Alone Together: How Marriage in America is Changing*, Harvard University Press, Cambridge, MA, 2006.
30. Radcliff Center, "Life's Work," Radcliff University, Work Policy Center, Cambridge, MA, 2000.
31. J. Gottman and R. Levenson, "Marital Happiness and Childrearing," *Marriage and Family*, Vol. 62, 2008, pp. 737–45.
32. E. Eaker, "Marital Strain and Risk of Heart Disease," *Psychosomatic Medicine*, July 2007, pp. 509–13.
33. J. Gottman and J. Gottman, *Ten Lessons to Transform Your Marriage*, Three Rivers, New York, 2007.

Chapter 7

1. Census Bureau, "Single Parent Households," US Department of Labor, Washington, DC, 2007.
2. J. Abbas, *Generation Ex: Adult Children of Divorce and the Healing of Our Pain*, Waterbrook Press, Boston, 2004.
3. C. Ahrons, *We're Still Family*, HarperCollins, New York, 2004.
4. P. Sobolewski and J. Amato, "Coparenting Relationships and Fathers' Ties to Children," in M.Lamb (ed.), *The Role of the Father in Child Development*, Wiley, New York, 2004, pp. 185–203.
5. L. Chadwick, "Absent Parents Are More Than Money," *Family Issues*, Vol. 64, 2002, pp. 661–65.
6. M. Conway, T. Christensen, and B. Herlihy, "Adult Children of Divorce and Intimate Relationships," *The Family Journal*, Vol. 11, 2003, pp. 364–73.
7. J. Harvey and M. Fine, *Children of Divorce*, Lawrence Erlbaum, New York, 2004.
8. M. Hetherington and J. Kelly, *For Better or Worse: Divorce Reconsidered*, Norton, New York, 2002.
9. J. Kelly and R. Emery, "Children's Adjustment Following Divorce," *Family Relations*, Vol. 52, 2003, pp. 352–62.
10. P. Kilmann, "Attachment Patterns for College Women of Intact vs. Non-intact Families," *Journal of Adolescence*, Vol. 29, 2006, pp. 89–102.
11. V. King, "Parental Divorce and Interpersonal Trust in Adult Offspring," *Journal of Marriage and Family*, Vol. 64, 2002, pp. 642–56.
12. V. Sobolewski and J. King, "Nonresident Fathers' Contributions to Adolescent Well-being," *Journal of Marriage and Family*, Vol. 68, 2006, pp. 537–57.
13. E. Marquardt, *Between Two Worlds: Inner Lives of Children of Divorce*, Crown, New York, 2005.
14. C. Menning, "Absent Parents Are More Than Money," *Journal of Family Issues*, Vol. 23, 2002, pp. 648–71.
15. H. Riggio, "Parental Divorce and Relationship Anxiety in Young Adulthood," *Personal Relationships*, Vol. 11, 2004, pp. 99–114.
16. S. Stewart, "Nonresident Parenting and Adolescent Adjustment," *Journal of Family Issues*, Vol. 24, 2003, pp. 217–44.
17. J. Wallerstein and S. Blakeslee, *What About the Kids?* Hyperion, New York, 2004.
18. S. Bailey and A. Zvonkovic, "Parenting After Divorce," *Journal of Divorce and Remarriage*, 2006, pp. 59–80.

19. N. Baum, "Post Divorce Paternal Disengagement," *Journal of Marriage and Family Therapy*, Vol. 32, 2006, pp. 245–54.
20. P. Bokker, R. Farley, and G. Denny, "Emotional Well Being Among Recently Divorced Fathers," *Journal of Divorce and Remarriage*, Vol. 41, 2005, pp. 157–72.
21. G. Stone, "Father Post Divorce Well-being," *Journal of Divorce and Remarriage*, Vol. 41, 2007, pp. 139–50.
22. W. Coleman, "Involving Fathers in Medical Care," *Pediatrics*, Vol. 113, 2004, pp. 1406–11.
23. J. Fagan and A. Hawkins, Clinical and Educational Interventions with Fathers, Haworth, New York, 2003.
24. B. Frieman, "Helping Professionals Understand Challenges of Non-custodial Parents," *Journal of Divorce and Remarriage*, Vol. 39, 2007, pp. 167–73.
25. F. Lin, "Adult Children's Support of Frail Parents," *Marriage and the Family*, 2008, pp. 44–52.
26. C. Ahrons, "Family Ties After Divorce," *Family Process*, Vol. 46, 2006, pp. 53–65.
27. M. Scott, A. Booth, and V. King, "Post Divorce Father-Adolescent Closeness," *Journal of Marriage and Family*, Vol. 94, 2007, pp. 1194–1209.
28. V. King, K Harris, and H. Heard, "Racial Diversity in Nonresident Father Involvement," *Journal of Marriage and the Family*, Vol. 66, 2004, pp. 1–21.
29. H. Frank, "Marital Status, Conflict and Post Divorce Predictors," *Journal of Divorce and Remarriage*, Vol. 39, 2004, pp. 105–24.
30. S. Fine and M. Harper, "Non-custodial Fathers Interactions with Children," *Fathering*, Vol. 4, 2006, pp. 286–311.
31. W. Fabricus, "Listening to Children of Divorce," *Family Relations*, Vol. 52, 2003, pp. 385–96.
32. G. Finley and S. Schwartz, "Father Involvement and Young Adult Outcomes," *Family Court Review*, Vol. 45, 2007, pp. 573–87.
33. D. Knox, M. Zusman, and A. DeCuzzi, "Effects of Divorce on Relationships with Parents," *College Student Journal*, Vol. 38, 2004, pp. 597–601.
34. J. Sobolewski and V. King, "Coparental Relationship and Nonresident Fathers' Ties to Children," *Journal of Marriage and Family*, Vol. 67, 2005, pp. 1196–1212.
35. J. Fields, "Children's Living Arrangements, US Department of Labor, Census Bureau, Washington, DC, 2003.

36. J. Kelly, "Children's Living Arrangements Following Divorce," *Family Process*, Vol. 46, 2007, pp. 35–52.

37. N. Grinnin, "Terms That Are Not Endearments," *New York Times*, December 12, 2004, A15.

38. J. Troilo and M. Coleman, "College Students' Perceptions of Father Stereotypes," *Marriage and the Family*, Vol. 70, 2008, pp. 218–27.

39. J. Gottman and J. Gottman, *Ten Lessons to Transform Your Marriage*, Three Rivers, New York, 2007.

40. Ibid.

41. S. Braver, *Divorced Dads: Shattering the Myths*, Putnam, New York, 1998.

42. M. Hallman and R. Deinhart, "Father's Experiences After Separation and Divorce," *Fathering*, Vol. 5, 2007, pp. 4–24.

43. W. Comanor (ed.), *The Law and Economics of Child Support Payments*, Edward Elgar, New York, 2004.

44. K. Folse and H. Varela, "Economic Consequences of Child Support for the Middle Class," *Journal of Socio-Economics*, Vol. 31, 2002, pp. 273–85.

45. C. Ahrons, *We're Still Family*, HarperCollins, New York, 2004.

46. M. Hetherington and J. Kelly, *For Better or Worse: Divorce Reconsidered*, Norton, New York, 2002.

47. S. Braver, J. Cookston, and B. Cohen, "Experiences of Family Law Attorneys with Current Divorce Practice," *Family Relations*, Vol. 51, 2002, pp. 325–34.

48. D. Dotterweich, "Attitudes Regarding Gender Bias in Child Custody Cases," *Family and Conciliation Courts Review*, Vol. 38, 2000, pp. 208–14.

49. J. Kelly and J. Johnston, "Problems with Custody Recommendations," *Family Court Review*, Vol. 43, 2005, pp. 88–93.

50. E. Kruk, "Shared Parental Responsibility," *Journal of Divorce and Remarriage*, Vol. 43, 2005, pp.119–40.

51. L. Stamps, "Age Difference Among Judges Regarding Child Custody Decisions," *Court Review*, Winter, 2002, pp. 18–22.

52. G. Williams, "Judicial Response to Joint Custody Statutes," Law and Society Conference, Las Vegas, 2007.

53. E. Douglas, *Mending Broken Families*, Rowman & Littlefield, New York, 2006.

54. J. Kelly, "Children's Living Arrangements Following Divorce," *Family Process*, Vol. 46, 2007, pp. 35–52.

55. R. Bauserman, "Child Adjustment in Joint-Custody Vs. Sole-Custody," *Journal of Family Psychology*, Vol. 16, 2002, pp. 91–102.

56. K. Breivik and D. Olweus, "Adolescent Adjustment in Post Divorce Families," *Journal of Divorce and Remarriage*, Vol. 39, 2007, pp. 400–15.

57. R. Emery, *The Truth About Children and Divorce*, Viking, New York, 2004.

58. R. Emery and R. Laumann, "Distress Among Young Adults from Divorced Families," *Journal of Family Psychology*, Vol. 14, 2000, pp. 671–87.

59. R.Warshak, *Divorce Poison*, Regan Books, New York, 2001.

60. L. Nielsen, "College Daughters' Relationships with Their Fathers: A Fifteen Year Study," *College Student Journal*, Vol. 54, 2006, pp. 16–30.

61. A. Smith, "Re-thinking Children's Involvement in Decision Making," *Family Law Journal*, Vol. 259, 2003, pp. 259–66.

62. K. Blaisure and M. Geasler, "Educational Interventions for Divorcing Parents and Their Children" in M. Fine and J. Harvey (eds.), *Handbook of Divorce and Relationship Dissolution*, Erlbaum, Mahway, New Jersey, 2006, 82–94.

63. D. Brandon, "Can Four Hours Make a Difference?" *Journal of Divorce and Remarriage*, Vol. 62, 2006, pp. 171–85.

64. S. Braver, J. Cookston, and W. Griffin, "Effects of the Dads for Life Intervention Program," *Family Process*, Vol. 46, 2007, pp. 123–37.

65. M. Criddle and M. Scott, "Mandatory Divorce Education and Post Divorce Parental Conflict," *Journal of Divorce and Remarriage*, Vol. 62, 2005, pp. 99–111.

66. M. Fine and F. Pei, "Evaluation of a Parenting Program for Divorcing Parents," *Journal of Divorce and Remarriage*, Vol. 62, 2005, pp. 1–23.

67. M. Pruett, G. Insabellla, and K. Gustafson, "Collaborative Divorce Project," *Family Court Review*, Vol. 43, 2005, pp. 38–51.

68. G. Stone, "Qualitative Evaluation of Parent Education Programs for Divorced Parents," *Journal of Divorce and Remarriage*, Vol. 62, 2006, pp. 25–40.

69. M. Toews and P. McKenry, "Predictors of Parenting Cooperation After Divorce," *Journal of Divorce and Remarriage*, Vol. 42, 2007, pp. 57–73.

70. A.F.C.C., "Planning for Shared Parenting," Association of Family and Conciliation Courts, Boston, 2006.

71. R. Warshak, "Blanket Restrictions: Overnight Contacts Between Parents and Young Children," *Family and Conciliation Courts Review*, Vol. 38, 2000, pp. 16–17.

72. W. Fabricus and S. Braver, "Divorced Parents' Financial Support of Their Children's College Expenses," *Family Court Review*, Vol. 41, 2003, pp. 145–56.

73. W. Fabricus and S. Braver, "Non-Child Support Expenditures on Children by Nonresidential Divorced Fathers," *Family Court Review*, Vol. 41, 2003, pp. 70–82.
74. W. Farrell, *Father and Child Reunion*, Tarcher, New York, 2001.
75. C. Buchanan and E. Maccoby, *Adolescents After Divorce*, Harvard University, Cambridge, MA, 1996.
76. R. Kelly, L. Redenbach, and W. Rinaman, "Determinants of Custody Arrangements in a National Sample," *American Journal of Family Law*, Vol. 19, 2005, pp. 25–43.
77. S. Schwartz and G. Finley, "Divorce Variables as Predictors of Young Adults Fathering Reports," Journal of Divorce and Remarriage, Vol. 44, 2005, pp. 144–64.
78. L. Weitzman, *The Divorce Revolution*, Free Press, Boston, 1985.
79. G. Duncan and S. Hoffman, "Reconsideration of Economic Consequences of Divorce," *Demographics*, Vol. 22, 1985, pp. 485–97.
80. S. Braver, *Divorced Dads: Shattering the Myths*, Putnam, New York, 1998.
81. K. Bonach, E. Sales, and G. Koeske, "Gender Differences in Co-parenting Quality," *Journal of Divorce and Remarriage*, Vol. 42, 2005, pp. 1–28.
82. M. Markham, L. Ganong, and M. Coleman, "Mothers' Cooperation in Coparental Relationships," *Family Relations*, Vol. 56, 2007, pp. 369–77.
83. K. Henley and K. Pasley, "Coparenting Following Divorce" in M. Fine and J. Harvey (eds.), *Handbook of Divorce*, Erlbaum, Mahway, NJ, 2006, pp. 241–62.
84. M. Markham, L. Ganong, and M. Coleman, "Mothers' Cooperation in Coparental Relationships," *Family Relations*, Vol. 56, 2007, pp. 369–77.
85. K. Henley and K. Pasley, "Coparenting Following Divorce" in M. Fine and J. Harvey (eds.), *Handbook of Divorce*, Erlbaum, Mahway, NJ, 2006, pp. 241–62.
86. A. Baker, *Adult Children of Parental Alienation Syndrome*, Norton, New York, 2007.
87. J. Clawar, *Children Held Hostage*, American Bar Association, Washington, DC, 2003.
88. D. Madden and S. Leonard, "Formerly Married Parents' Perceptions of Custody," *Family Relations*, Vol. 51, 2002, pp. 37–45.
89. A. Baker, *Adult Children of Parental Alienation Syndrome*, Norton, New York, 2007.

90. J. Clawar, *Children Held Hostage*, American Bar Association, Washington, DC, 2003.

91. J. Kelly, "Children's Living Arrangements Following Divorce," Family Process, Vol. 46, 2007, pp. 35–52.

92. R. Coley, "What Mothers Teach, What Daughters Learn" in A. Crouter and A. Booth (eds.), *Just Living Together*, Erlbaum, Mahweh, NJ, 2002, pp. 97–196.

93. A. Gallion, *No More Baby's Mama Drama*, Kensington, New York, 2005.

94. D. Hollister, "Baby Mama Drama," Hip-O Records, 2006.

95. M. Stevens, "Why Can't We Be Friends: A Black Man's Thoughts on How to End Baby Mama Drama," SSC Training, Baltimore, MD, 2006.

96. J. Laasko, "Fathering in Low Income Single Parent Families," Fathering,Vol. 2, 2004, pp. 131–45.

97. W. Johnson, "Black Fathers," *Journal of Marriage and Family*, Vol. 44, 2007, pp. 67–78.

98. A. Leite and P. McHenry, "Nonresident Father Involvement," Fathering, Vol. 4, 2006, pp. 21–35.

99. P. England and K. Edin, *Unmarried Couples with Children*, Russell Sage Foundation, New York, 2007.

Chapter 8

1. S. Bowling and R. Werner, "Father Daughter Relationships and Adolescent Female Sexuality," *Journal of HIV/AIDS Prevention*, Vol. 3, 2000, pp. 5–28.

2. M. Hutchinson, "Communication Between Parents and Daughters on Sexual Risk Behaviors," Family Relations, Vol. 51, 2002, pp. 238–47.

3. B. Bates, J. Dodge, and K. Ellis, "Father Absence and Teenage Pregnancy," Child Development, Vol. 74, 2003, pp. 801–21.

4. R. Quinlan, "Father Absence and Female Reproductive Development," Evolution and Human Behavior, Vol. 24, 2007, pp. 376–90.

5. A. Schalet, Raging Hormones, Regulated Love, University of Chicago, Chicago, 2006.

6. A.G.I, Sex and America's Teenagers, Alan Guttmacher Institute, New York, 2006.

7. M. Regnerus, Forbidden Fruit: Sex and Religion in Lives of American Teenagers, Oxford University Press, New York, 2007.

8. M. Miller and J. Lee, "Communicating Disappointment," *Journal of Family Communications*, Vol. 1, 2001, pp. 111–31.

9. Census Bureau, "Recent Trends in Pregnancy," Department of Labor, Washington, DC, 2006.
10. Ibid.
11. M. Reumann, *American Sexual Character*, University of California, Berkeley, CA, 2003.
12. N S.I, *American Sexual Behavior*, NSI Press, New York, 2006.
13. Ibid
14. A.G.I, *Abortion in the U.S.*, Alan Guttmacher Institute, New York, 2008.
15. Ibid.
16. K. Bogle, *Hooking Up: Sex and Relationships on Campus*, New York University, New York, 2008.
17. P. England and R. Thomas, "Rise of the College Hook Up" in D. Skolnick (ed.), *Families in Transition*, Allyn Bacon, Boston, 2006, pp. 56–79.
18. J. Arnett, *Emerging Adulthood*, Prentice Hall, Englewood Cliffs, NJ, 2006.

Chapter 9

1. K. Taylor, *Black Fathers*, Doubleday, New York, 2003.
2. O. Clayton, R. Mincy, and W. Blankenhorn, *Black Fathers in Contemporary Society*, Russell Sage, New York, 2006.
3. A. Hattery and E. Smith, *African American Families*, Sage, Los Angeles, 2008.
4. Ibid.
5. Ibid.
6. Census Bureau, "Single Parent Households," Department of Labor, Washington, DC, 2007.
7. P. England and K. Edin, *Unmarried Couples with Children*, Russell Sage Foundation, New York, 2007.
8. J. Barras, *Whatever Happened to Daddy's Little Girl*, Ballantine, New York, 2000.
9. ———, *Bridges: Reuniting Daughters and Daddies*, Bancroft, Baltimore, MD, 2005.
10. ———, *Whatever Happened to Daddy's Little Girl*, Ballantine, New York, 2000.
11. ———, *Bridges: Reuniting Daughters and Daddies*, Bancroft, Baltimore, MD, 2005.
12. R. King, *Papa Was a Rolling Stone*, Read 4 Life, Coralville, IA, 2007.
13. M. Beaty, *My Soul to His Spirit: Expressions from Black Daughters to Their Fathers*, Soul Dictates, Alsip, IL, 2007.

14. Ibid.

15. Ibid.

16. J. Hamer, *What It Means to Be Daddy*, Columbia University, New York, 2001.

17. J. Fagan and A. Hawkins, *Clinical and Educational Interventions with Fathers*, Haworth, New York, 2003.

18. G. Stone and J. Dudley, *Fathering at Risk: Helping Non-residential Fathers*, Men's Studies Press, Harriman, TN, 2006.

19. H. Garson, *Oprah Winfrey: A Biography*, Greenwood Press, Nashville, TN, 2004.

Index